Simple Solutions

Solving Problems in Math Education!

Level 5

Nancy L. McGraw

Bright Ideas Press
Cleveland Heights, Ohio

Simple Solutions *Level 5*

Printed in the United States of America

ISBN: 0-9728730-2-3

Cover Design: Tim Naujoks
Editor: Kimberly A. Dambrogio, NBCT

Welcome to

Simple Solutions

Note to the Student:

This workbook will give you the opportunity to practice skills you have learned in previous grades. By practicing these skills each night, you will gain confidence in your math ability.

Using this workbook will help you understand math concepts easier and for many of you, it will give you a more positive attitude toward math in general.

In order for this program to help you be successful, it is extremely important that you do every lesson every night. It is also important that you ask your teacher for help on the problems you don't understand or get wrong when checking your homework.

If you put forth the effort, I guarantee that Simple Solutions will change your opinion about math forever.

Lesson #1

1. 45,263 + 29,577 = ?

2. Find the median of 64, 56 and 88.

3. Draw 2 congruent pentagons.

4. Find the average of 65, 75 and 70.

5. It is 4:15. What time was it six hours ago?

6. 7,000 – 3,556 = ?

7. How many feet are in a mile?

8. Draw an obtuse angle.

9. 5,344 × 7 = ?

10. Which digit is in the thousands place in 386,419?

11. The answer to a subtraction problem is called the _____.

12. 3,656 ÷ 6 = ?

13. What is the name of this shape?

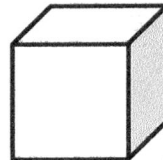

14. Draw a horizontal line.

15. 45 × 24 = ?

16. How many dimes are in a dollar?

17. Round 56,213 to the nearest ten thousand.

18. Write the next number in the sequence. 46, 51, 56, …

19. How many cups are in a pint?

20. List the even numbers between 81 and 89.

1.	2.	3.	4.
5.	6.	7.	8.
9.	10.	11.	12.
13.	14.	15.	16.
17.	18.	19.	20.

Lesson #2

1. How many quarts are in 5 gallons?

2. Draw perpendicular lines.

3. Write 4,622 in expanded form.

4. $263,455 + 198,663 = ?$

5. Find the range of 86, 19, 25, 76 and 35.

6. A telephone would best be weighed in ounces or in pounds?

7. $8,654 \times 5 = ?$

8. A six-sided polygon is called a(n) _____.

9. $306 \div 6 = ?$

10. $703 - 159 = ?$

11. The answer to a division problem is called the _____.

12. Round 6,215,446 to the nearest thousand.

13. $3,762 \bigcirc 3,672$

14. How many months is it from June 1st to October 1st?

15. $4.6 + 2.3 = ?$

16. It is 3:10. What time will it be in 4 hours and 15 minutes?

17. The top number in a fraction is called the _____.

18. $\dfrac{2}{5} + \dfrac{1}{5} = ?$

19. Put $\dfrac{4}{12}$ in simplest form.

20. Identify the type of angle.

1.	2.	3.	4.
5.	6.	7.	8.
9.	10.	11.	12.
13.	14.	15.	16.
17.	18.	19.	20.

Lesson #3

1. How many cups are in 5 pints?

2. $45 \times 23 = ?$

3. Draw intersecting lines.

4. $3,466 + 9,512 = ?$

5. Find the perimeter of this figure.

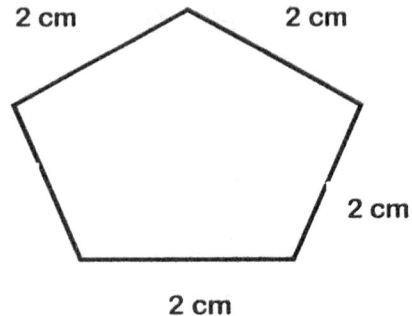

2 cm   2 cm

2 cm   2 cm

2 cm

6. Put $\dfrac{5}{15}$ in simplest form.

7. Which digit is in the hundred thousands place in 365,217?

8. How many grams are in a kilogram?

9. How many degrees are in a right angle?

10. $60,000 - 25,415 = ?$

11. $465 \div 25 = ?$

12. $\dfrac{4}{5} = \dfrac{?}{15}$

13. $56 + 24 + 81 = ?$

14. Two decades before 1952 was what year?

15. If the diameter of a circle is 12 cm, what is the radius?

16. Write the standard number for $50,000 + 4,000 + 200 + 60 + 1$.

17. Find the average of 11, 87 and 19.

18. Draw a pentagon.

19. What is the bottom number in a fraction called?

20. Mark is 3 years older than Susan. Susan is 4 years younger than Monica. Monica is 15. How old is Mark?

1.	2.	3.	4.
5.	6.	7.	8.
9.	10.	11.	12.
13.	14.	15.	16.
17.	18.	19.	20.

Lesson #4

1. $5,490 \div 3 = ?$

2. How many ounces are in 3 pounds?

3. Round 2,416,304 to the nearest million.

4. $\dfrac{4}{9} - \dfrac{2}{9} = ?$

5. Find the median of 36, 14, 21, 56 and 10.

6. $957 \div 78 = ?$

7. Write 6.2 using words.

8. How many yards are in a mile?

9. $7,280 \times 9 = ?$

10. A closed figure made up of line segments is called a(n) _____.

11. Find the perimeter of the triangle shown above.

12. It is 2:00. What time was it 4 hours and 15 minutes ago?

13. $4,216 - 1,775 = ?$

14. Put $\dfrac{6}{9}$ in simplest form.

15. $4.7 - 2.9 = ?$

16. $\dfrac{4}{5} = \dfrac{8}{?}$

17. What fraction is shaded?

18. Draw an acute angle.

19. A glass would weigh about 75 grams or 75 kilograms?

20. The answer in a multiplication problem is called the _____.

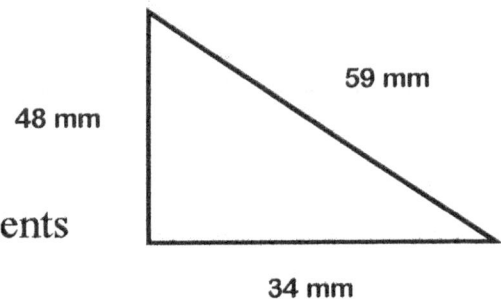

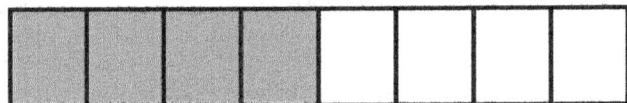

1.	2.	3.	4.
5.	6.	7.	8.
9.	10.	11.	12.
13.	14.	15.	16.
17.	18.	19.	20.

Lesson #5

1. How many pints are in a quart?

2. $39 + 27 + 10 = ?$

3. $321 \times 25 = ?$

4. Draw a ray.

5. Write the next number in the sequence. 86, 79, 72, …

6. If the radius of a circle is 10 mm, what is the diameter?

7. Round 875,233 to the nearest ten thousand.

8. Find the average of 160, 121 and 151.

9. $14,580 \div 9 = ?$

10. Draw a right angle.

11. $500 - 163 = ?$

12. Carlos sold 12 bottles of perfume at $48.00 each. How much money did he make selling perfume?

13. A four-sided polygon is called a(n) _____.

14. Write the odd numbers between 70 and 76.

15. Find the area of this square.

16. Ninety years is _____ decades.

17. Put $\dfrac{12}{15}$ in simplest form.

6 m

18. $86.25 - 17.6 = ?$

19. $\dfrac{4}{7} + \dfrac{2}{7} = ?$

20. Write 'nine and twenty-three hundredths' as a decimal number.

1.

2.

3.

4.

5.

6.

7.

8.

9.

10.

11.

12.

13.

14.

15.

16.

17.

18.

19.

20.

Lesson #6

1. $\dfrac{5}{7} = \dfrac{?}{35}$

2. The sum is the answer to a(n) _____ problem.

3. The top number in a fraction is called the _____.

4. Draw a line segment.

5. Find the range of 98, 13, 41, 62 and 8.

6. Figures with the same size and shape are _____.

7. Put $\dfrac{8}{12}$ in simplest form.

8. Name the shape.

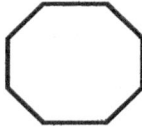

9. $14{,}237 \times 3 = ?$

10. Write 341,257 in expanded form.

11. A penny would weigh about a gram or a kilogram?

12. $42{,}089 \div 8 = ?$

13. 600 years are how many centuries?

14. *There are 1,000 millimeters in 1 meter.* Write '1,000 mm = 1 m' three times.

15. What is the probability of getting heads on one flip of a coin?

16. How many teaspoons are in 4 tablespoons?

17. $3.74 + 6.9 = ?$

18. $\dfrac{2}{7} + \dfrac{3}{7} = ?$

19. $374{,}219 + 455{,}667 = ?$

20. How many inches of snow fell in 1967? How much more snow fell in 1967 than in 1972?

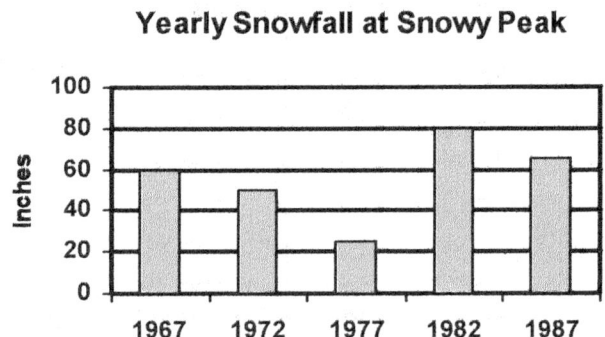

Yearly Snowfall at Snowy Peak

1.	2.	3.	4.
5.	6.	7.	8.
9.	10.	11.	12.
13.	14.	15.	16.
17.	18.	19.	20.

Lesson #7

1. Draw a horizontal line.

2. $396 \div 82 = ?$

3. John is 4 feet 8 inches tall. What is his height in inches?

4. $516,677 + 78,918 = ?$

5. $12 \times 12 = ?$

6. Find the area.

9 ft

2 ft

7. Write 'six and four tenths' as a decimal number.

8. Put $\dfrac{5}{10}$ in simplest form.

9. Write $\dfrac{8}{6}$ as a mixed number.

10. $8,000 - 2,444 = ?$

11. Find the median of 16, 94, 66, 29 and 40.

12. If it is 12:40 now, what time will it be in 5 hours and 10 minutes?

13. How many yards are in a mile?

14. Draw 2 similar squares.

15. $\dfrac{8}{9} - \dfrac{3}{9} = ?$

16. $57 \div 7 = ?$

17. $3,214 \bigcirc 3,412$

18. Find the average of 320, 294, 265 and 301.

19. $36 + \underline{\quad} = 82$

20. List the even numbers between 51 and 58.

1.	2.	3.	4.
5.	6.	7.	8.
9.	10.	11.	12.
13.	14.	15.	16.
17.	18.	19.	20.

Lesson #8

1. How many millimeters are in a meter?

2. Write 7.23 using words.

3. How many minutes are in 4 hours?

4. The distance across a circle, through the center, is the _____.

5. $3,127 - 1,769 = ?$

6. Which digit is in the ten thousands place in 567,812?

7. A pentagon has _____ sides.

8. Draw perpendicular lines.

9. Write the standard number for $80,000 + 6,000 + 300 + 90$.

10. $9.2 + 6.9 = ?$

11. Put $\dfrac{4}{8}$ in simplest form.

12. $325 \times 213 = ?$

13. $\dfrac{8}{9} = \dfrac{?}{27}$

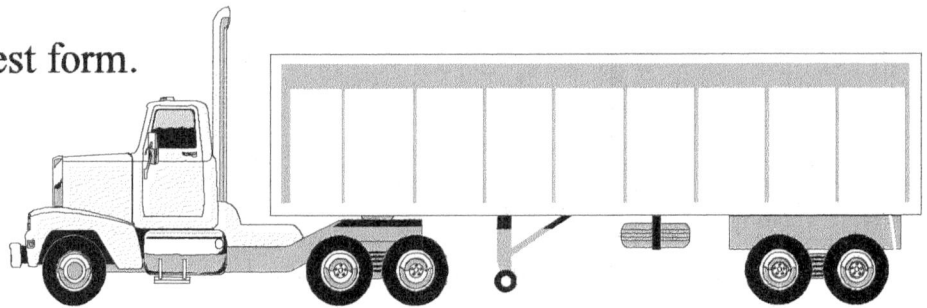

14. Write the next two numbers in the sequence. 66, 74, 82, …

15. $\dfrac{7}{10} - \dfrac{4}{10} = ?$

16. Round 86,215 to the nearest hundred.

17. What is the name of the shape to the right?

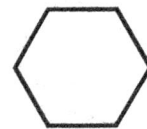

18. An angle less than 90° is called a(n) _____ angle.

19. *A straight angle is a line. Its measure is 180°.*
    Draw a straight angle and label it 180°.

20. If a truck weighs 4 tons, how many pounds does it weigh?

1.	2.	3.	4.
5.	6.	7.	8.
9.	10.	11.	12.
13.	14.	15.	16.
17.	18.	19.	20.

Lesson #9

1.   Find the perimeter of the figure.   6 cm

3 cm

2.   Jeff had 5 quarters, 2 dimes and 4 pennies. How much money did Jeff have?

3. $80,000 - 46,556 = ?$

4.   Is this figure a polygon?

5.   Two figures with the same shape, but with different sizes are ____.

6. $396 \div 82 = ?$

7.   Write the decimal number 'seventeen and seven hundredths.'

8. $47,598 + 61,323 = ?$

9.   How many feet are in 4 yards?

10. $325 \times 132 = ?$

11. How many degrees are in a straight angle?

12. $75 - \underline{\quad} = 36$

13. What will be the time 8 minutes before 2:00?

14. Draw a hexagon.

15. Which digit is in the hundred thousands place in 2,671,835?

16. $\dfrac{7}{12} - \dfrac{5}{12} = ?$

17. How many millimeters are in a meter?

18. $18.23 + 7.6 = ?$

1 METER

19. Put $\dfrac{4}{16}$ in simplest form.

20. $\dfrac{4}{6} = \dfrac{?}{24}$

1.	2.	3.	4.
5.	6.	7.	8.
9.	10.	11.	12.
13.	14.	15.	16.
17.	18.	19.	20.

Lesson #10

1. $1,007 - 698 = ?$

2.   Classify each angle below as acute, right, obtuse or straight.

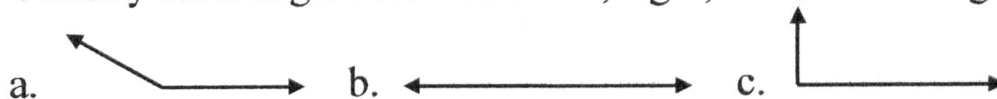

      a.   b.   c.

3. $1,407 \div 7 = ?$

4.   Find the average of 1,121, 1,087 and 1,095.

5.   Give the name of this shape.

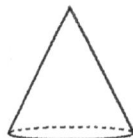

6.   Write 10.9 using words.

7.   If the radius of a circle is 8 cm, what is the diameter?

8. $60 \times 40 = ?$

9. $\dfrac{2}{10} + \dfrac{3}{10} = ?$

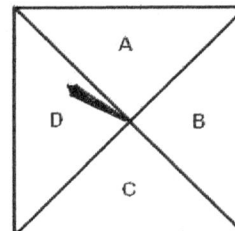

10.   What is the probability of the spinner landing on a D?

11.   Nancy bought 8 golf balls for $24. How much
      would she have to pay for 12 golf balls?

12. $32,804 \times 3 = ?$

13.   Write $\dfrac{9}{7}$ as a mixed number.

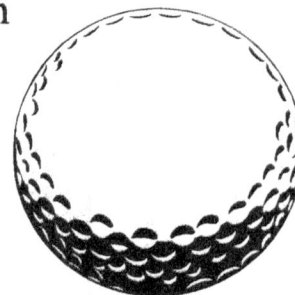

14.   How many months are in 3 years?

15.   Round 896,275 to the nearest hundred thousand.

16.   What fraction of the triangle is not shaded?

17.   Which is longer 3 feet or 3 yards?

18.   Draw intersecting lines.

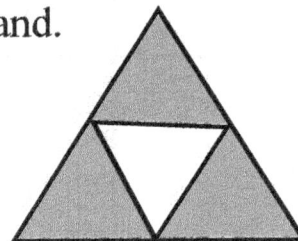

19.   Put $\dfrac{10}{15}$ in simplest form.

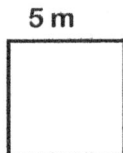

20.   Find the area of the square.

5 m

1.

2.

3.

4.

5.

6.

7.

8.

9.

10.

11.

12.

13.

14.

15.

16.

17.

18.

19.

20.

Lesson #11

1. The movie began at 7:30 and lasted 90 minutes. At what time did the movie end?

2. Write $6\dfrac{2}{5}$ as an improper fraction.

3. $60,275 + 24,845 = ?$

4. Draw a line segment.

5. $4,823 \div 23 = ?$

6. How many inches are in a yard?

7. Will a can of pop hold about 350 milliliters or 350 liters?

8. $125 \times 214 = ?$

9. Write $\dfrac{9}{5}$ as a mixed number.

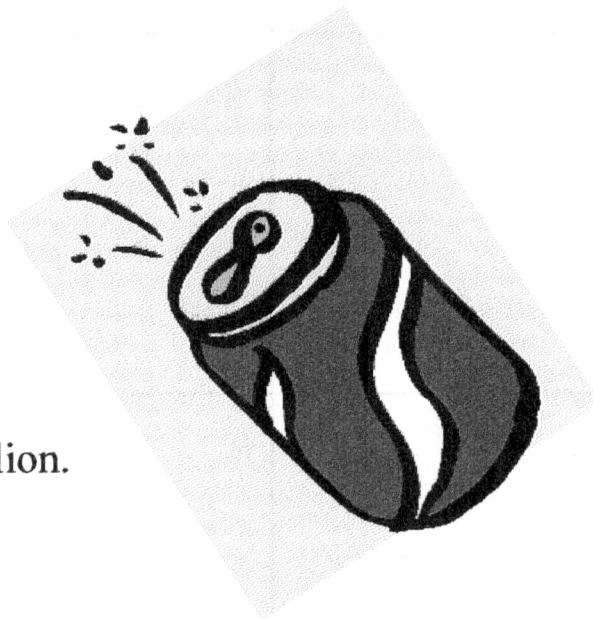

10. $\dfrac{5}{8} = \dfrac{?}{16}$

11. $6.25 + 7.36 = ?$

12. Round 9,816,075 to the nearest million.

13. $\dfrac{5}{7} + \dfrac{2}{7} = ?$

14. $34,214 \times 7 = ?$

15. Draw a square. Draw a line of symmetry through the square.

16. Write the standard number for $8,000 + 600 + 40 + 4$.

17. How many grams are in a kilogram?

18. $641 - 259 = ?$

19. Find the range of 42, 38, 14 and 66.

20. How many cookies are in 5 dozen cookies?

1.

2.

3.

4.

5.

6.

7.

8.

9.

10.

11.

12.

13.

14.

15.

16.

17.

18.

19.

20.

Lesson #12

1. Any four-sided polygon is called a(n) _____.

2. $2,884 \div 14 = ?$

3. Draw an acute angle.

4. $425 + 663 = ?$

5. Which is heavier, 6 grams or 6 kilograms?

6. $96 \times 36 = ?$

7. How many nickels are in a dollar?

8. Round 1,365,212 to the nearest ten thousand.

9. $\dfrac{1}{4} + \dfrac{1}{4} = ?$

10. What is $\dfrac{1}{2}$ of 50?

11. Put $\dfrac{3}{9}$ in simplest form.

12. What was the year two centuries before 1986?

13. Find the average of 135, 375 and 450.

14. Write 'three and twenty-seven hundredths' as a decimal.

15. $\dfrac{3}{4} = \dfrac{9}{?}$

16. Find the perimeter of this polygon.

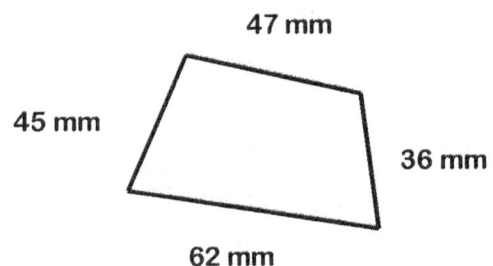

17. $5,050 - 1,385 = ?$

18. How many degrees are in a straight angle?

19. There are _____ millimeters in a meter.

20. *On the Fahrenheit temperature scale, water freezes at 32°F and it boils at 212°F. Write 'Fahrenheit freezing = 32°F' and 'Fahrenheit boiling = 212°F'.*

1.	2.	3.	4.
5.	6.	7.	8.
9.	10.	11.	12.
13.	14.	15.	16.
17.	18.	19.	20.

Lesson #13

1. Write $\dfrac{12}{5}$ as a mixed number.

2. $\dfrac{5}{8} - \dfrac{1}{8} = ?$

3. Find the area.

   11in.

   6 in.

4. What is the probability of getting a 2 on one roll of a die?

5. In Fahrenheit, water boils at_____.

6. How many teaspoons are in 5 tablespoons?

7. Write 'twelve and two hundredths' as a decimal.

8. $841,263 + 977,455 = ?$

9. Round 8,314,205 to the nearest million.

10. Draw an obtuse angle.

11. $324 \times 213 = ?$

12. Are these shapes congruent?

13. Would a gasoline tank hold about 40 ml or 40 L of gasoline?

14. $5,121 - 3,677 = ?$

15. List the factors of 12.

16. How many decades are 40 years?

17. $8,452 \div 4 = ?$

18. Is 13 a prime or a composite number?

19. Which digit is in the hundred thousands place in 7,342,815?

20. Find $\dfrac{1}{5}$ of 25.

1.	2.	3.	4.
5.	6.	7.	8.
9.	10.	11.	12.
13.	14.	15.	16.
17.	18.	19.	20.

Lesson #14

1. Put $\dfrac{4}{6}$ in simplest form.

2. $86 \times 52 = ?$

3. What will be the time 45 minutes after midnight?

4. $43,204 - 19,561 = ?$

5. The pear would more likely weigh 200 grams or 200 kilograms?

6. $13.7 - 10.5 = ?$

7. How many centimeters are in 3 meters?

8. Is 24 a prime or a composite number?

9. $55 + 13 + 8 = ?$

10. $\dfrac{9}{10} - \dfrac{2}{10} = ?$

11. $865 \div 25 = ?$

12. Draw a line of symmetry through this oval.

13. In Fahrenheit, water freezes at _____.

14. Find the perimeter.

8 m
4 m   4 m
4 m

15. Marsha is 6 feet 2 inches tall. What is Marsha's height in inches?

16. List the factors of 24.

17. $\dfrac{5}{9} = \dfrac{?}{36}$

18. Any four-sided figure is called a(n) _____.

19. Find the average of 75, 93, 88 and 60.

20. What kind of angle measures less than 90°?

1.

2.

3.

4.

5.

6.

7.

8.

9.

10.

11.

12.

13.

14.

15.

16.

17.

18.

19.

20.

Lesson #15

1. How many degrees are in a straight angle?

2. $633,215 + 45,866 = ?$

3. Would a cupcake best be
    weighed in ounces or in pounds?

4. Put $\dfrac{3}{12}$ in simplest form.

5. List the factors of 18.

6. $125 \times 216 = ?$

7. What is the probability of rolling a number greater than 4 on one
    roll of a die?

8. Find the area.

    8 cm

    16 cm

9. $27.9 - 13.2 = ?$

10. Find the range of 37, 76, 53 and 25.

11. $720 \div 3 = ?$

12. Round 6,414,862 to the nearest thousand.

13. Water boils at what temperature on the Fahrenheit scale?

14. Is this figure a polygon?

15. Write 56,214 in expanded form.

16. $60,000 - 15,833 = ?$

17. How many days are in 2 years?

18. If the radius of a circle is 12 meters, what is its diameter?

19. Draw a right angle. How many degrees are in a right angle?

20. Is the dotted line a line of symmetry in the arrow?

1.	2.	3.	4.
5.	6.	7.	8.
9.	10.	11.	12.
13.	14.	15.	16.
17.	18.	19.	20.

Lesson #16

1. $8,036 \div 4 = ?$

2. What are the first 4 prime numbers?

3. Find the median of 37, 18, 56, 49 and 20.

4. $70 \times 30 = ?$

5. How many millimeters are in a meter?

6. List the factors of 14.

7. $302 - 179 = ?$

8. The answer to a subtraction problem is called the _____.

9. Write $\dfrac{11}{5}$ as a mixed number.

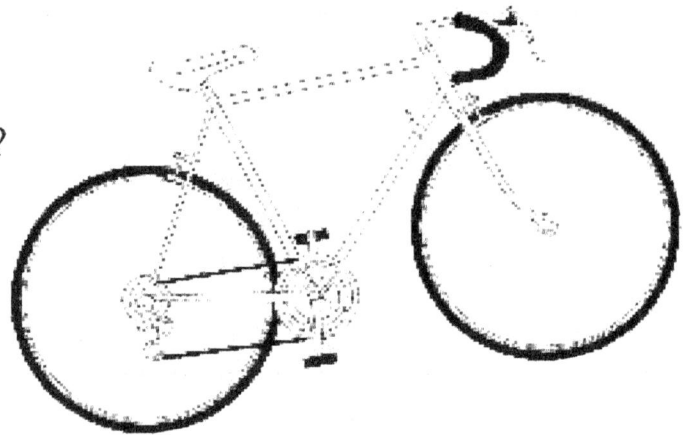

10. How many feet are in 2 miles?

11. $\dfrac{2}{6} + \dfrac{3}{6} = ?$

12. Draw 2 congruent circles.

13. $88,016 + 38,937 = ?$

14. Find the average of 87, 91, 95, 92 and 85.

15. $\dfrac{5}{9} \bigcirc \dfrac{7}{8}$

16. Write $4\dfrac{2}{5}$ as an improper fraction.

17. It is 9:30. What time will it be in 10 hours?

18. Put $\dfrac{3}{6}$ in simplest form.

19. Which digit is in the millions place in 8,419,206?

20. Would a bike weigh 10 grams or 10 kilograms?

1.	2.	3.	4.
5.	6.	7.	8.
9.	10.	11.	12.
13.	14.	15.	16.
17.	18.	19.	20.

Lesson #17

1. $8.2 + 9.6 = ?$

2.   Put $\dfrac{8}{16}$ in simplest form.

3. $36,842 - 19,689 = ?$

4.   How many yards are in a mile?

5.   What's the probability of rolling an even number on 1 roll of a die?

6.   Find the average of 1,124, 723 and 859.

7. $295 \div 14 = ?$

8.   Is 19 a prime number or a composite number?

9.   Find the perimeter of a pentagon, if the sides each measure 6 inches.

10. $\dfrac{9}{10}$ $\bigcirc$ $\dfrac{3}{4}$

11. Two figures with the same shape, but different sizes are _____.

12. List the factors of 15.

13. $47 \times 93 = ?$

14. On the Fahrenheit scale, water freezes at _____.

15. Would the length of a pair of pliers best be measured in inches or in feet?

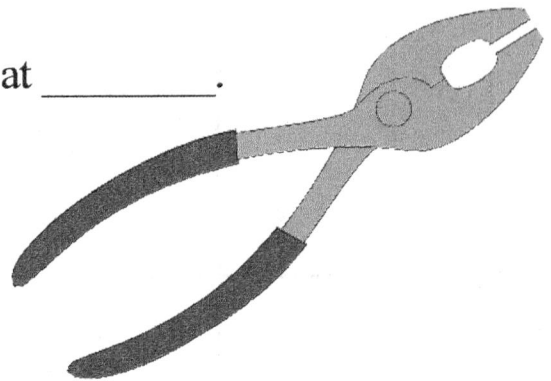

16. Show a line of symmetry.

17. $\dfrac{3}{7} = \dfrac{?}{49}$

18. The quotient is the answer to a(n) _____ problem.

19. Identify the shape by name.

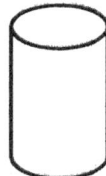

20. Write $\dfrac{6}{4}$ as a mixed number.

1.	2.	3.	4.
5.	6.	7.	8.
9.	10.	11.	12.
13.	14.	15.	16.
17.	18.	19.	20.

Lesson #18

1. List the factors of 10.

2. What is the area of the rectangle?

   8 cm

   5 cm

3. $\dfrac{3}{4}$ ◯ $\dfrac{7}{8}$

4. How many feet are in 4 yards?

5. $97,316 + 29,407 = ?$

6. Find the range of 81, 16, 43, 98 and 11.

7. Draw a ray.

8. How many millimeters are in 4 meters?

9. Is 25 a prime or a composite number?

10. $90,000 - 36,642 = ?$

11. How many degrees are in a straight angle?

12. Find the greatest common factor (GCF) of 10 and 15.

13. $324 \times 22 = ?$

14. The distance that is half of the diameter is called the _____.

15. A hexagon has _____ sides.

16. Put $\dfrac{5}{10}$ in simplest form.

17. $4,535 \div 5 = ?$

18. Write the next number in the sequence. 34, 41, 48, …

19. Write the standard number for $500,000 + 60,000 + 3,000 + 300.$

20. Find the perimeter.

    4 in.

    9 in.

1.

2.

3.

4.

5.

6.

7.

8.

9.

10.

11.

12.

13.

14.

15.

16.

17.

18.

19.

20.

Lesson #19

1. $66 \times 23 = ?$

2. Draw a line of symmetry through the arrow.

3. On the Fahrenheit scale, water boils at _____ .

4. $3,888 \div 36 = ?$

5. $1,006 - 599 = ?$

6. Write 'sixteen and five tenths' as a decimal.

7. $34,175 \times 5 = ?$

8. Find the median of 62, 40, 25, 96 and 15.

9. $\dfrac{6}{7} - \dfrac{1}{7} = ?$

10. $82,730 + 5,896 = ?$

11. List the factors of 16.

12. Round 87,342,119 to the nearest million.

13. $\dfrac{3}{4} \bigcirc \dfrac{4}{5}$

14. How many cups are in 4 pints?

15. Find the greatest common factor (GCF) of 12 and 18.

16. Is 48 a prime number or a composite number?

17. How many ounces are in 6 pounds?

18. Put $\dfrac{12}{15}$ in simplest form.

19. Write $6\dfrac{1}{3}$ as an improper fraction.

20. What is the coldest time of day? How many degrees did the temperature rise between 8:30 a.m. and noon?

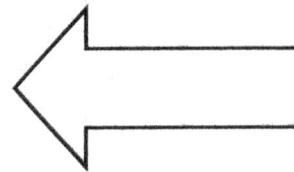

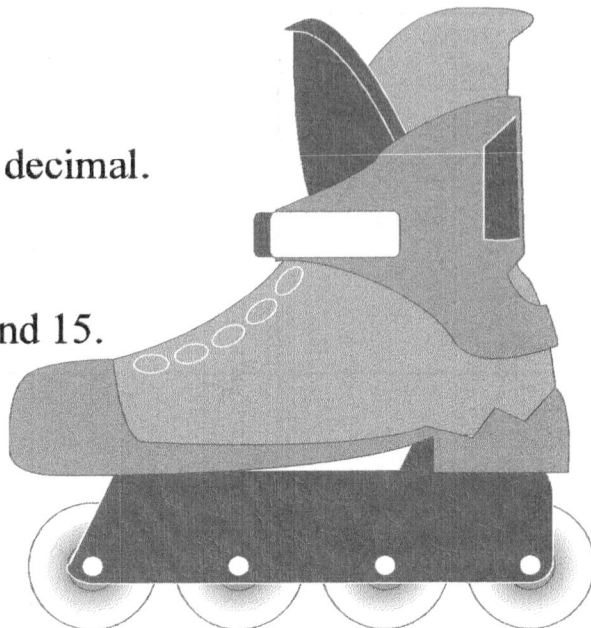

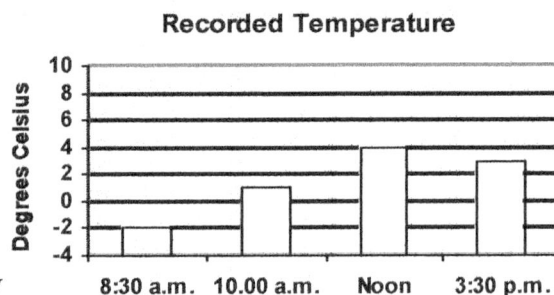

1.

2.

3.

4.

5.

6.

7.

8.

9.

10.

11.

12.

13.

14.

15.

16.

17.

18.

19.

20.

Lesson #20

1.   If the radius of a circle is 10 cm, what is its diameter?

2. $769,213 + 86,754 = ?$

3.   Give the probability of rolling a prime number on one roll of a die?

4.   Find the area of the quadrilateral.

5.   Draw perpendicular lines.

7 in.

7 in.

6. $331 \times 25 = ?$

7. $9,000 - 6,331 = ?$

8.   Find the greatest common factor (GCF) of 12 and 16.

9.   Which digit is in the hundred thousands place in 5,367,402?

10. It is 5:35. What time was it 4 hours and 15 minutes ago?

11. Find the average of 320, 294, 265 and 301.

12. Put $\dfrac{5}{20}$ in simplest form.

13. An eight-sided polygon is called a(n) _____.

14. $5,760 \div 8 = ?$

15. How many feet are in 3 miles?

16. Are these figures similar?

17. List the factors of 24.

18. How many weeks are 84 days?

19. $\dfrac{5}{8} = \dfrac{30}{?}$

20. A store has 176 televisions to sell. If they sell 86 televisions one day and 49 the next day, how many televisions are left to be sold?

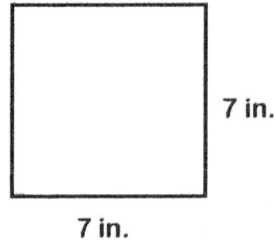

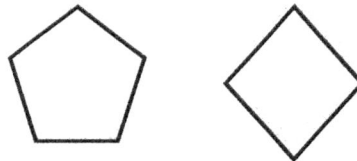

1.	2.	3.	4.
5.	6.	7.	8.
9.	10.	11.	12.
13.	14.	15.	16.
17.	18.	19.	20.

Lesson #21

1. Find the GCF of 9 and 12.

2. $23,843 \div 4 = ?$

3. Draw intersecting lines.

4. A right angle measures _____ degrees.

5. List the factors of 14.

6. $46 + 24 + 13 = ?$

7. $85 \times 53 = ?$

8. How many years are 7 centuries?

9. What will be the time 10 minutes before 1:00?

10. Find the area.

    5 cm

    7 cm

11. Is 13 a prime or a composite number?

12. $\dfrac{5}{6} \bigcirc \dfrac{2}{3}$

13. The answer to a multiplication problem is called the _____.

14. List the even numbers between 60 and 70.

15. $4.6 - 1.7 = ?$

16. How many pints are in a quart?

17. Round 7,887,530 to the nearest thousand.

18. Figures with the same size and shape are _____.

19. Identify the type of angle.

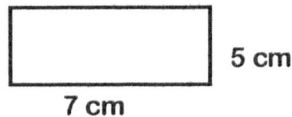

20. How many quarters have the same value as $2?

1.	2.	3.	4.
5.	6.	7.	8.
9.	10.	11.	12.
13.	14.	15.	16.
17.	18.	19.	20.

Lesson #22

1. How many millimeters are in 4 meters?

2. $\dfrac{9}{10} \bigcirc \dfrac{7}{8}$

3. $\dfrac{4}{5} + \dfrac{1}{5} = ?$

4. If a baby weighs 80 ounces. What is the baby's weight in pounds?

5. Find the least common multiple (LCM) of 9 and 12.

6. *On the Celsius scale, water freezes at 0°C and boils at 100°C.* Write 'Celsius freezing = 0°C' and 'Celsius boiling = 100°C.'

7. List the factors of 18.

8. Identify the name of this shape.

9. $48 + \underline{\quad} = 83$

10. Liquid in an eyedropper is best measured in milliliters or in liters?

11. Put $\dfrac{6}{18}$ in simplest form.

12. $12 \times 12 = ?$

13. Draw a line segment.

14. If it is 2:55 now, what time was it 3 hours and 20 minutes ago?

15. Write 6.21 using words.

16. Half of a circle's diameter is called its $\underline{\quad\quad}$.

17. $6{,}219 - 3{,}988 = ?$

18. How many feet are in 5 yards?

19. $973 \div 54 = ?$

20. Jason is 3 years younger than Thomas. Thomas is 2 years older than George. If George is 14, how old is Jason?

1.	2.	3.	4.
5.	6.	7.	8.
9.	10.	11.	12.
13.	14.	15.	16.
17.	18.	19.	20.

Lesson #23

1. $29,676 \div 4 = ?$

2. Draw a ray.

3. A five-sided polygon is called a(n) _____.

4. In Celsius, water freezes at _____.

5. $\dfrac{5}{7} \bigcirc \dfrac{7}{8}$

6. Round 5,887,116 to the nearest hundred thousand.

7. $47 \times 22 = ?$

8. Find the median of 37, 19 and 50.

9. Which is longer, a meter or a kilometer?

10. $418,233 + 86,504 = ?$

11. Are these shapes similar or congruent?

12. $\dfrac{5}{6} = \dfrac{?}{36}$

13. Which digit is in the millions place in 46,075,312?

14. A plane weighs 3 tons. How many pounds does the plane weigh?

15. List the factors of 15.

16. Put $\dfrac{5}{25}$ in simplest form.

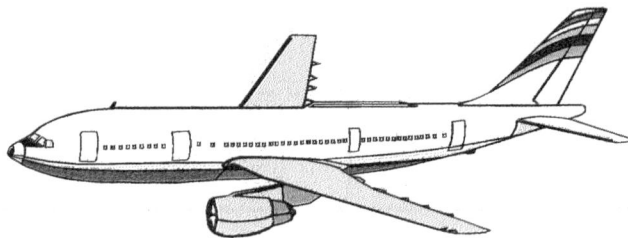

17. $60,000 - 28,199 = ?$

18. Find the least common multiple (LCM) of 8 and 15.

19. Write the first four prime numbers.

20. Find the perimeter of the square.

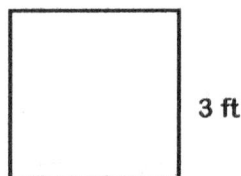

3 ft

1.	2.	3.	4.
5.	6.	7.	8.
9.	10.	11.	12.
13.	14.	15.	16.
17.	18.	19.	20.

Lesson #24

1. Find the GCF of 15 and 25.

2. How many teaspoons are in 7 tablespoons?

3. Would a bag of popcorn weigh about 900 grams or 900 kilograms?

4. $5 \times 5 \times 3 = ?$

5. Write 31,226 in expanded form.

6. $6.32 + 15.8 = ?$

7. Draw a line of symmetry.

8. $\dfrac{3}{4} \bigcirc \dfrac{2}{3}$

9. On the Celsius scale, water boils at _____.

10. $455 \times 32 = ?$

11. How many yards are in 2 miles?

12. $4,102 - 1,667 = ?$

13. Sean is 5 feet 7 inches tall. What is Sean's height in inches?

14. List the factors of 20.

15. $72,095 \div 45 = ?$

16. Write $5\dfrac{2}{3}$ as an improper fraction.

17. What time will it be in 90 minutes, if it is 7:00 now?

18. Put $\dfrac{3}{15}$ in simplest form.

19. Draw parallel, horizontal lines.

20. What is the probability that the spinner will land on a vowel? On the letter B?

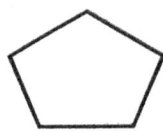

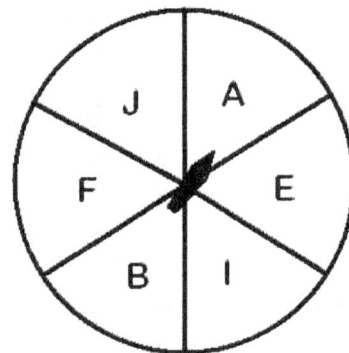

1.	2.	3.	4.
5.	6.	7.	8.
9.	10.	11.	12.
13.	14.	15.	16.
17.	18.	19.	20.

Lesson #25

1. Write $\dfrac{12}{7}$ as a mixed number.

2. $56{,}304 + 27{,}138 = ?$

3. Put $\dfrac{8}{12}$ in simplest form.

4. $\dfrac{3}{5} \bigcirc \dfrac{6}{7}$

5. Draw a hexagon.

6. Find the least common multiple (LCM) of 16 and 18.

7. $503 - 175 = ?$

8. Would the length of a car be about 4 meters or 4 kilometers?

9. List the factors of 25.

10. Find $\dfrac{1}{6}$ of 24.

11. Find the area.

```
        4 ft
   ┌──────────┐
   │          │ 2 ft
   └──────────┘
```

12. How many meters are 600 centimeters?

13. $15{,}345 \times 6 = ?$

14. Make a factor tree for 24.

15. Closed figures made up of line segments are called _____.

16. $18{,}345 \div 3 = ?$

17. Give the Celsius and Fahrenheit freezing temperatures of water.

18. Round 374,816 to the nearest ten thousand.

19. *The number that occurs most often in a set of numbers is called the mode.* Find the mode of 86, 39, 27, 39 and 80.

20. How many grams are in 7 kilograms?

1.

2.

3.

4.

5.

6.

7.

8.

9.

10.

11.

12.

13.

14.

15.

16.

17.

18.

19.

20.

Lesson #26

1. $16,464 \div 4 = ?$

2. Find the area of the rectangle.

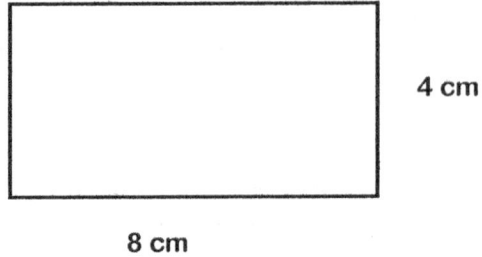

4 cm

8 cm

3. $\dfrac{8}{9} \bigcirc \dfrac{6}{7}$

4. Find $\dfrac{1}{7}$ of 49.

5. $6,429 + 8,552 = ?$

6. Draw an acute angle.

7. $20,000 - 9,335 = ?$

8. Is 23 a prime or a composite number?

9. Which digit is in the thousands place in 7,815,042?

10. How many cups are in 3 pints?

11. $551 \times 32 = ?$

12. Write 'twenty-five and three hundredths' as a decimal.

13. Find the Least Common Multiple (LCM) of 8 and 14.

14. $\dfrac{3}{4} = \dfrac{?}{20}$

15. The answer to an addition problem is called the _____.

16. Put $\dfrac{7}{35}$ in simplest form.

17. Would a dog weigh about 15 ounces or 15 pounds?

18. Are these lines perpendicular?

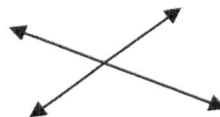

19. List the factors of 20.

20. Make a factor tree for 72.

1.	2.	3.	4.
5.	6.	7.	8.
9.	10.	11.	12.
13.	14.	15.	16.
17.	18.	19.	20.

Lesson #27

1. Find the area.

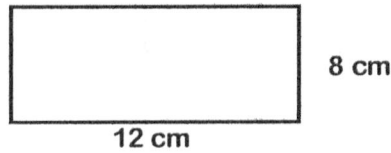

2. $\dfrac{8}{9} - \dfrac{3}{9} = ?$

8 cm

12 cm

3. Find the mode in 14, 25, 55, 14 and 62.

4. Find the median of the set of numbers in problem #3.

5. Make a factor tree for 45.

6. $183,214 + 88,752 = ?$

7. How many quarts are in 8 gallons?

8. $3,255 \times 4 = ?$

9. Draw an obtuse angle.

10. $20,000 - 6,431 = ?$

11. If a bus weighs 7 tons. What is its weight in pounds?

12. Put $\dfrac{6}{24}$ in simplest form.

13. Write $\dfrac{13}{7}$ as a mixed number.

14. How many ounces are in 4 pounds?

15. At what temperature does water boil on the Fahrenheit scale?

16. Find the GCF of 14 and 21.

17. Write $7\dfrac{4}{5}$ as an improper fraction.

18. $532 \div 21 = ?$

19. $235.76 - 97.8 =$

20. Are these shapes congruent or similar?

1.	2.	3.	4.
5.	6.	7.	8.
9.	10.	11.	12.
13.	14.	15.	16.
17.	18.	19.	20.

Lesson #28

1. The distance across the middle of a circle is called the _____.

2. $4 \times 28 = ?$

3. Find $\dfrac{1}{3}$ of 18.

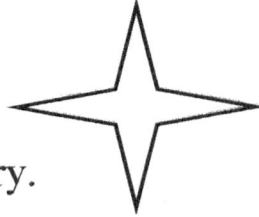

4. Find 2 lines of symmetry.

5. Find the perimeter of the triangle.

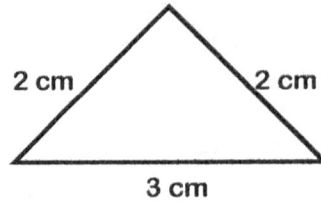

6. $23,513 - 18,658 = ?$

7. A key is about 5 centimeters or 5 meters long?

8. Round 32,415,266 to the nearest thousand.

9. Put $\dfrac{10}{15}$ in simplest form.

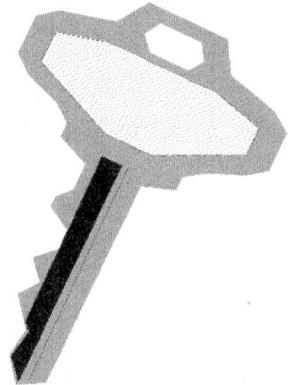

10. $8,604 \bigcirc 8,406$

11. $281 + 48 = ?$

12. Make a factor tree for 12.

13. Find the average of 1,121, 1,087 and 1,095.

14. Which digit is in the ten thousands place in 25,740?

15. $4,155 \div 5 = ?$

16. Write $5\dfrac{2}{5}$ as an improper fraction.

17. Identify the type of angle.

18. $\dfrac{2}{4} \bigcirc \dfrac{4}{8}$

19. $9.8 + 6.3 = ?$

20. What is the probability of landing on an even number? On a number greater than 1?

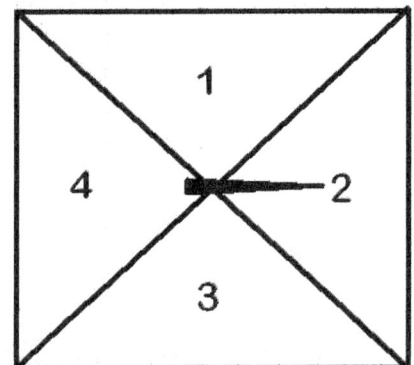

1.	2.	3.	4.
5.	6.	7.	8.
9.	10.	11.	12.
13.	14.	15.	16.
17.	18.	19.	20.

Lesson #29

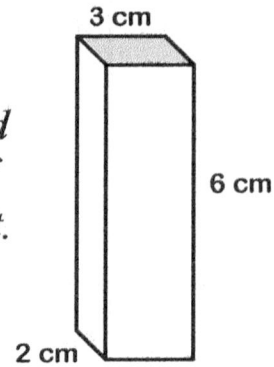

1.   Find the average of 87, 85 and 98.

2.   *Volume is a measure of space inside of a solid figure. The formula for finding the volume of a rectangular prism is length x width x height. (L x W x H)* Find the volume of this figure.

3 cm

6 cm

2 cm

3. $976 \div 6 = ?$

4.   If the radius of a circle is 14 cm, what is the diameter?

5. $300 \times 600 = ?$

6.   Put $\dfrac{25}{30}$ in simplest form.

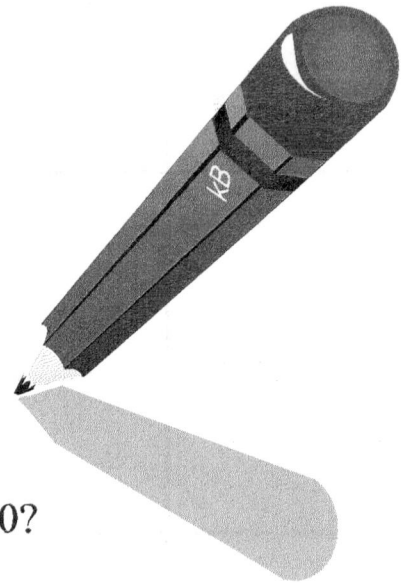

7.   List the factors of 21.

8. $4,000 - 885 = ?$

9.   Draw a ray.

10. Make a factor tree for 32.

11. What will be the time 80 minutes after 5:00?

12. $163,214 + 79,456 = ?$

13. $\dfrac{7}{10} \bigcirc \dfrac{8}{9}$

14. Find the GCF and the LCM of 12 and 16.

15. A five-sided polygon is called a(n) _____.

16. How many yards are in a mile?

17. Write the first 3 prime numbers.

18. $\dfrac{4}{7} = \dfrac{16}{?}$

19. Write $7,000 + 500 + 50 + 2$ as a standard number.

20. How many weeks are in 8 months?

1.	2.	3.	4.
5.	6.	7.	8.
9.	10.	11.	12.
13.	14.	15.	16.
17.	18.	19.	20.

Lesson #30

1. A bag of peanuts weighs about 600 grams or 600 kilograms?

2. List the Celsius and Fahrenheit boiling temperatures of water.

3. Find the mode of 33, 59, 86, 24 and 59.

4. $83 \times 38 = ?$

5. How many inches are in 3 feet?

6. $600,000 - 432,864 = ?$

7. Find the volume of this solid.

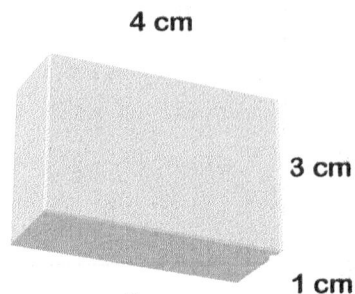

8. How many teaspoons are in 9 tablespoons?

9. Make a factor tree for 56.

10. $\dfrac{8}{9} + \dfrac{1}{9} = ?$

11. $3,963 \div 36 = ?$

12. $864 + 399 = ?$

13. Find the perimeter of the square.

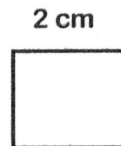

14. It is 1:25. What time will it be in 6 hours and 20 minutes?

15. An angle that measures more than 90° is called _____.

16. Put $\dfrac{4}{8}$ in simplest form.

17. How many pints are in 8 quarts?

18. Which is longer, 8 yards or 8 feet?

19. Find the range of 100, 92, 87 and 51.

20. Write $\dfrac{10}{3}$ as a mixed number.

1.	2.	3.	4.
5.	6.	7.	8.
9.	10.	11.	12.
13.	14.	15.	16.
17.	18.	19.	20.

Lesson #31

1. Find $\frac{1}{3}$ of 27.

2. $363,225 + 88,726 = ?$

3. Draw a line segment.

4. Find the volume of the cube.

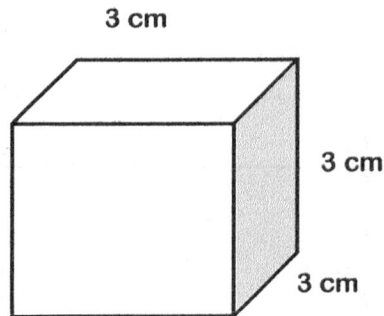

5. $40 \times 37 = ?$

3 cm

3 cm

3 cm

6. Is the number 36 prime or composite?

7. $7.3 - 5.7 = ?$

8. $63 + \underline{\quad} = 74$

9. Put $\frac{10}{25}$ in simplest form.

10. It is 3:05. What time was it 4 hours ago?

11. On the Celsius scale, water freezes at $\underline{\quad}$.

12. How many minutes are in 5 hours?

13. Would water in a bathtub best be measured in milliliters or in liters?

14. List the factors of 24.

15. $8,346 \div 6 = ?$

16. Draw perpendicular lines.

17. Make a factor tree for 40.

18. What is the GCF of 15 and 20?

19. Write the odd numbers between 20 and 28.

20. What is the probability of getting heads on one flip of a coin?

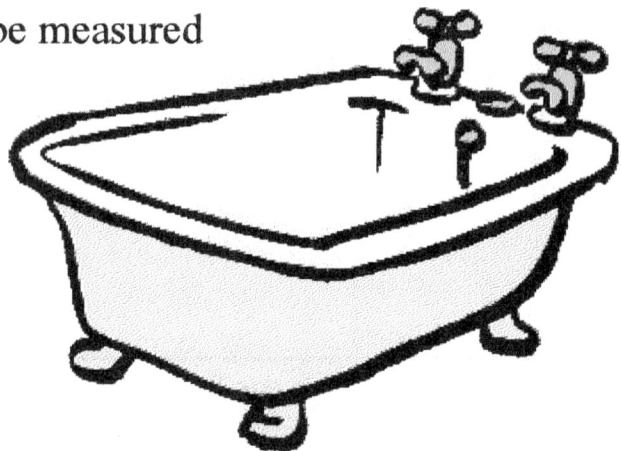

1.	2.	3.	4.
5.	6.	7.	8.
9.	10.	11.	12.
13.	14.	15.	16.
17.	18.	19.	20.

Lesson #32

1.   Any four-sided polygon is called a(n) _____.

2.   Put $\dfrac{14}{16}$ in simplest form.

3.   Round 16,244,336 to the nearest ten thousand.

4. $37 \times 81 = ?$

5.   List the factors of 18.

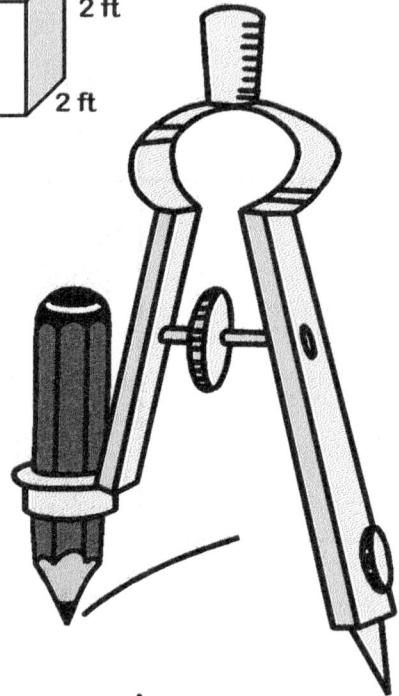

6. $46.3 + 10.75 = ?$

7.   Find the volume of the prism.

8.   Fifty years are _____ decades.

9. $137,216 + 886,774 = ?$

10. Closed figures made up of line segments are called _____.

11. Find the mode in 86, 41, 32, 41 and 75.

12. Draw a straight angle. How many degrees are in a straight angle?

13. $40,000 - 18,215 = ?$

14. The answer to a division problem is the _____.

15. How many inches are in 4 feet?

16. Find the LCM of 15 and 18.

17. $\dfrac{7}{9} - \dfrac{2}{9} = ?$

18. Numbers with only 2 factors are _____ numbers.

19. $6,543 \div 3 = ?$

20. Write $\dfrac{17}{5}$ as a mixed number.

1.

2.

3.

4.

5.

6.

7.

8.

9.

10.

11.

12.

13.

14.

15.

16.

17.

18.

19.

20.

Lesson #33

1. Find the GCF of 12 and 15.

2. Write 'seventeen and one hundredth' as a decimal.

3. Write the first 5 prime numbers.

4. $\dfrac{7}{15} - \dfrac{1}{15} = ?$

5. How many degrees are in a right angle?

6. Write $6\dfrac{2}{3}$ as an improper fraction.

7. $267,314 + 562,471 = ?$

8. Find the average and the mode of 271, 298 and 271.

9. $37,650 \div 5 = ?$

10. If the radius of a circle is 8 inches, what is the diameter?

11. What is the name this shape?

12. How many weeks are 105 days?

13. $348 \times 24 = ?$

14. Round 56,219,045 to the nearest million.

15. $302 - 89 = ?$

16. An angle that measures less than 90° is called _____.

17. Find the area of a square whose sides measure 10 cm.

18. Find the median of 18, 37, 96, 55 and 23.

19. Write the formula for finding the volume of a rectangular solid.

20. Twice a week, Steve works an 8-hour day for $7.00 per hour. Three days a week, he works a 7-hour a day for $5.00 per hour. How much does he earn each week?

1.	2.	3.	4.
5.	6.	7.	8.
9.	10.	11.	12.
13.	14.	15.	16.
17.	18.	19.	20.

Lesson #34

1. $\dfrac{9}{16} - \dfrac{5}{16} = ?$

2. Find the LCM of 6 and 15.

3. Write the even numbers between 30 and 38.

4. Find $\dfrac{1}{7}$ of 56.

5. $75,000 - 26,312 = ?$

6. Put $\dfrac{3}{18}$ in simplest form.

7. How many feet are in 4 miles?

8. Write $\dfrac{19}{7}$ as a mixed number.

9. A five-sided polygon is called a(n) _____.

10. Find the volume of the prism to the right.

11. The distance across a circle, through the center, is the _____.

12. On the Fahrenheit scale water freezes at_____.

13. Which digit is in the hundred thousands place in 46,780,213?

14. How many cups are in 5 pints?

15. List the factors of 14.

16. $685 \div 35 = ?$

17. $44 + 16 + 28 = ?$

18. Find the range of 103, 119, 110, 152 and 174.

19. $25,614 \times 4 = ?$

20. Find the perimeter of a rectangle whose length is 7 cm and whose width is 4 cm.

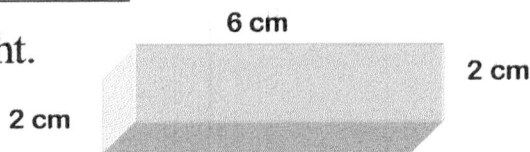

6 cm

2 cm

2 cm

1.	2.	3.	4.
5.	6.	7.	8.
9.	10.	11.	12.
13.	14.	15.	16.
17.	18.	19.	20.

Lesson #35

1. Draw a heart. Show a line of symmetry.

2. How many centimeters are 6 meters?

3. Put $\dfrac{4}{24}$ in simplest form.

4. $93 \times 37 = ?$

5. If it is 4:45 now, what time was it 5 hours and 15 minutes ago?

6. The answer to a multiplication problem is the _____.

7. Draw perpendicular lines.

8. What is the probability of rolling an odd number on one roll of a die?

9. $\dfrac{5}{7} = \dfrac{?}{21}$

10. How many quarters are in $4.00?

11. Write $40,000 + 5,000 + 30 + 5$ as a standard number.

12. How many months is it from January 1st to April 1st?

13. $3.6 + 4.9 = ?$

14. Write $3\dfrac{2}{3}$ as an improper fraction.

15. Would yogurt best be measured in milliliters or liters?

16. Find the GCF of 12 and 18.

17. How many feet are in 6 yards?

18. Write 15.9 using words.

19. $41,315 - 28,569 = ?$

20. List the factors of 20.

1.	2.	3.	4.
5.	6.	7.	8.
9.	10.	11.	12.
13.	14.	15.	16.
17.	18.	19.	20.

Lesson #36

1. What will be the time 80 minutes after noon?

2. $47,245 \div 5 = ?$

3. Put $\dfrac{2}{6}$ in simplest form.

4. $\dfrac{4}{6} + \dfrac{2}{6} = ?$

5. Trisha is 4 feet 8 inches tall. What is Trisha's height in inches?

6. How many degrees are in a straight angle?

7. Round 4,657 to the nearest hundred.

8. $13,506 \times 6 = ?$

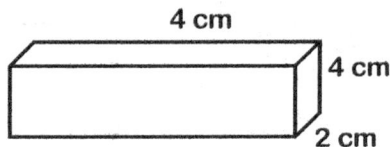

9. Find the volume of the prism.

10. A jet weighs 8 tons. How many pounds does a jet weigh?

11. Draw intersecting lines.

12. A(n) _____ has six sides.

13. Find the area of a square whose sides each measure 8 mm.

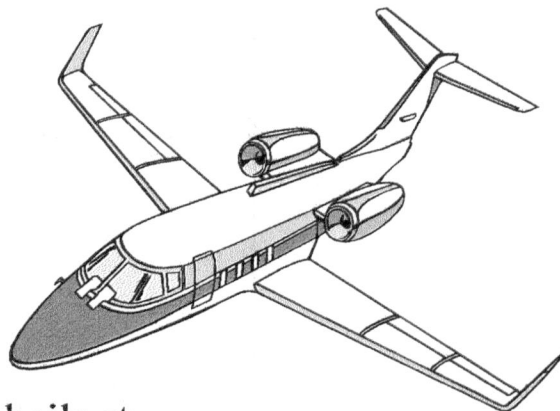

14. Write $4\dfrac{1}{2}$ as an improper fraction.

15. On a Fahrenheit thermometer, water boils at _____.

16. $\dfrac{4}{7} \bigcirc \dfrac{5}{8}$

17. How many millimeters are in 3 meters?

18. $20,000 - 8,316 = ?$

19. $456 \div 24 = ?$

20. Two figures with the same size and shape are _____.

1.

2.

3.

4.

5.

6.

7.

8.

9.

10.

11.

12.

13.

14.

15.

16.

17.

18.

19.

20.

Lesson #37

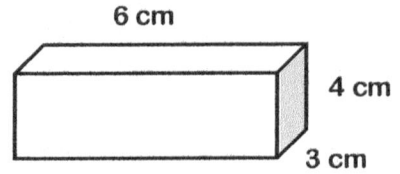

6 cm
4 cm
3 cm

1. Find the volume of this rectangular solid.

2. Draw a right angle.

3. Find the LCM of 9 and 14.

4. The Celsius freezing temperature of water is _____.

5. What is the probability of rolling a number greater than 2 on one roll of a die?

6. $345,119 + 762,344 = ?$

7. Numbers with only 2 factors are called _____ numbers.

8. $\dfrac{5}{7} \bigcirc \dfrac{9}{10}$

9. Write 'six and two tenths' as a decimal.

10. $806 - 279 = ?$

11. How many feet are in 4 yards?

12. $374 \times 22 = ?$

13. A television set would best be weighed in grams or in kilograms?

14. List the factors of 16.

15. $6,020 \div 6 = ?$

16. Put $\dfrac{8}{12}$ in simplest form.

17. Find the average of 18, 25, 15, 29 and 18.

18. Write $\dfrac{14}{3}$ as a mixed number.

19. Half of the diameter of a circle is called the _____.

20. $\dfrac{3}{5} + \dfrac{1}{2} = ?$

1.

2.

3.

4.

5.

6.

7.

8.

9.

10.

11.

12.

13.

14.

15.

16.

17.

18.

19.

20.

Lesson #38

1. Draw perpendicular lines.

2. Find the perimeter of a square if the length of a side is 7 feet.

3. $60,000 - 38,515 = ?$

4. Round 7,866,213 to the nearest hundred thousand.

5. Find the GCF of 12 and 18.

6. How many feet are in 2 miles?

7. $7.1 + 21.6 = ?$

8. $\dfrac{3}{4} + \dfrac{1}{3} = ?$

9. Put $\dfrac{8}{24}$ in simplest form.

10. $748 \div 63 = ?$

11. Write $6\dfrac{3}{7}$ as an improper fraction.

12. $13,642 \times 3 = ?$

13. Make a factor tree for 42.

14. Find the range of 31, 86, 92, 14 and 100.

15. Draw two similar squares.

16. How many centimeters are in 8 meters?

17. $\dfrac{4}{5} \bigcirc \dfrac{6}{8}$

18. A quadrilateral has _____ sides.

19. Which digit is in the ten thousands place in 457,302?

20. Find the volume of the figure.

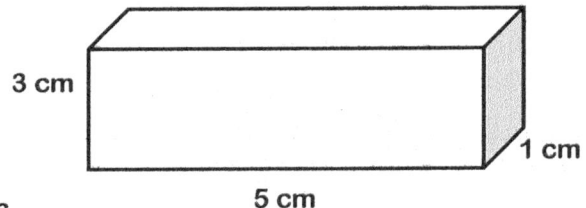

3 cm

1 cm

5 cm

1.	2.	3.	4.
5.	6.	7.	8.
9.	10.	11.	12.
13.	14.	15.	16.
17.	18.	19.	20.

Lesson #39

1.   If it is 5:10 now, what time will it be in 4 hours and 20 minutes?

2. $\dfrac{3}{7} + \dfrac{1}{3} = ?$

3.   Draw an obtuse angle.

4. $88 \times 34 = ?$

5.   Is this figure a polygon?

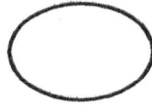

6.   Find the area of the quadrilateral.

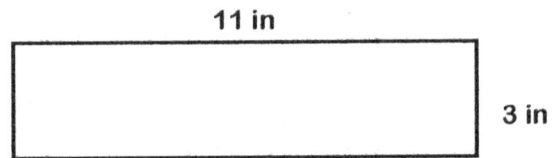

7. $97 \div 23 = ?$

8.   Find the LCM of 6 and 15.

9.   Is 56 a prime or a composite number?

10. How many millimeters are in 9 meters?

11. $331 + 469 = ?$

12. If the diameter of a circle is 16 cm, what is the radius?

13. How many dimes are in $3.00?

14. $\dfrac{4}{9} = \dfrac{?}{27}$

15. Write $5\dfrac{1}{7}$ as an improper fraction.

16. Find the mode of 37, 55, 18, 37 and 62.

17. List the factors of 20.

18. How many ounces are in 4 pounds?

19. Make a factor tree for 64.

20. The _____ is the answer in a subtraction problem.

1.	2.	3.	4.
5.	6.	7.	8.
9.	10.	11.	12.
13.	14.	15.	16.
17.	18.	19.	20.

Lesson #40

1. $\dfrac{3}{8} + \dfrac{1}{4} = ?$

2. An angle that measures less than 90° is called _____.

3. Write the time 7 minutes before 3:00.

4. Find the volume of the solid to the right.

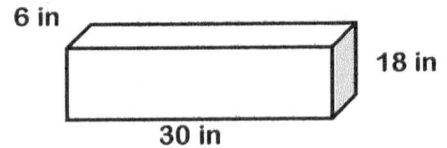

5. Round 38,204,516 to the nearest thousand.

6. $5,382 \div 26 = ?$

7. Write $\dfrac{15}{2}$ as a mixed number.

8. Draw a pentagon.

9. Find the median of 37, 48, 10, 19 and 41.

10. Write the odd numbers between 50 and 58.

11. Put $\dfrac{15}{20}$ in simplest form.

12. $800 \times 600 = ?$

13. How many pints are in 3 quarts?

14. $\dfrac{9}{11} \bigcirc \dfrac{8}{9}$

15. $34,818 + 28,963 = ?$

16. Mark bought a notebook for $1.59, some filler paper for $0.89 and 3 pens at $0.49 each. How much did Mark spend on supplies?

17. Draw parallel, horizontal lines.

18. Write 16.31 using words.

19. $801 - 667 = ?$

20. What is the probability that the spinner will land on an even number? A number greater than 3?

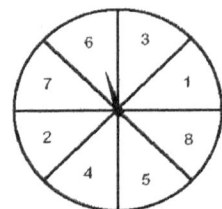

1.	2.	3.	4.
5.	6.	7.	8.
9.	10.	11.	12.
13.	14.	15.	16.
17.	18.	19.	20.

Lesson #41

1. How many seconds are in 7 minutes?

2. Find the GCF of 8 and 16.

3. $51 + 18 + 7 = ?$

4. Round 5,304,298 to the nearest hundred.

5. Allie is 3 years younger than Karen. Karen is 4 years older than Jessica. Jessica is 12. How old is Allie?

6. The answer in a multiplication problem is called the ____.

7. List the factors of 12.

8. Write $9\frac{2}{9}$ as an improper fraction.

9. $43,215 \times 5 = ?$

10. Find the average of 48, 72, 48, 83 and 49.

11. How many degrees are in a straight angle?

12. Draw intersecting lines.

13. The boiling temperature of water, in Celsius, is _____.

14. Find the area of a square whose sides each measure 8 inches.

15. Write 32,616 in expanded form.

16. $\frac{5}{6} + \frac{2}{3} = ?$

17. How many pounds are 6 tons?

18. $30,000 - 19,471 = ?$

19. Sixty years are _____ decades.

20. $10,545 \div 5 = ?$

1.	2.	3.	4.
5.	6.	7.	8.
9.	10.	11.	12.
13.	14.	15.	16.
17.	18.	19.	20.

Lesson #42

1. $15 \times 6 = ?$

2. It is 5:35. What time will it be in 2 hours and 25 minutes?

3. Draw a vertical line.

4. $787,156 + 156,324 = ?$

5. $50 \div 8 = ?$

6. $6,318 - 4,756 = ?$

7. An eight-sided polygon is a(n) _____.

8. How many feet are in a mile?

9. Find $\dfrac{1}{5}$ of 35.

10. $4,675 \bigcirc 4,764$

11. Put $\dfrac{7}{21}$ in simplest form.

12. $5\dfrac{5}{7} + \dfrac{2}{3} = ?$

13. Gary was the ninth person in line. How many people were in front of him?

14. How many centuries are the same as 400 years?

15. Write 4,567 in expanded form.

16. Make a factor tree for 30.

17. Tina is 5 feet 4 inches tall. What is Tina's height in inches?

18. On the Fahrenheit scale, water freezes at _____.

19. Write the next 2 numbers in the sequence. 12, 18, 24, ...

20. Hank has 56 books. He wants to put them into equal piles with 8 books in each pile. How many piles of books will he have?

1.	2.	3.	4.
5.	6.	7.	8.
9.	10.	11.	12.
13.	14.	15.	16.
17.	18.	19.	20.

Lesson #43

1. Harry lives 12 blocks from school. How many blocks does Harry walk when he walks to school and back home?

2. $18 + \underline{\quad} = 78$

3. Find the volume of the figure. 3 cm 5 cm 1 cm

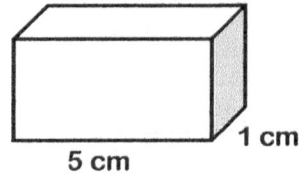

4. $57 \times 43 = ?$

5. Would a baseball bat best be weighed in grams or in kilograms?

6. $1\dfrac{4}{5} + 2\dfrac{1}{3} = ?$

7. Write the first four prime numbers.

8. $21,416 - 8,377 = ?$

9. Draw 2 congruent hexagons.

10. The top number in a fraction is called the _____.

11. How many seconds are in 2 hours?

12. $45,065 \div 5 = ?$

13. Find $\dfrac{1}{3}$ of 21.

14. Round 5,203,776 to the nearest million.

15. Find the average of 45, 78, 23 and 86.

16. $\dfrac{7}{8} \bigcirc \dfrac{3}{4}$

17. Find the GCF of 8 and 12.

18. How many grams are in 8 kilograms?

19. List the factors of 24.

20. Write 12.07 using words.

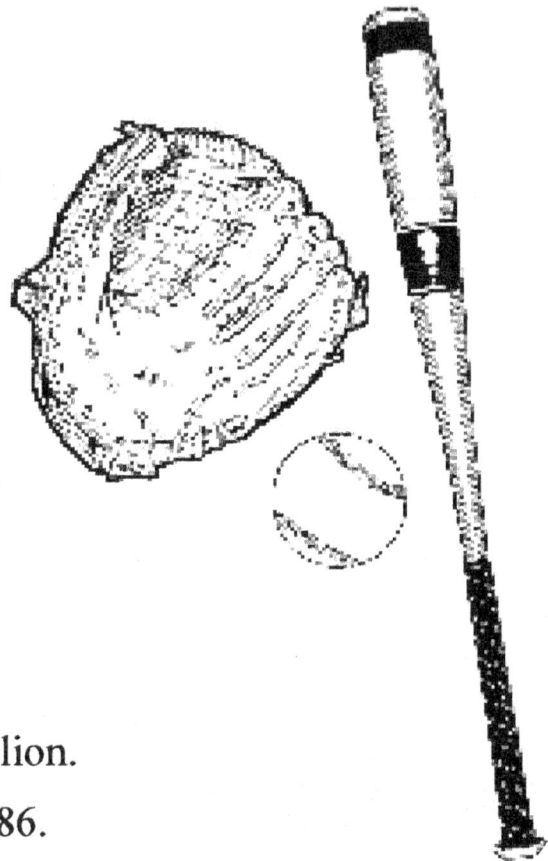

1.	2.	3.	4.
5.	6.	7.	8.
9.	10.	11.	12.
13.	14.	15.	16.
17.	18.	19.	20.

Lesson #44

1. $80 - \underline{\quad} = 25$

2. Draw a ray.

3. Round 458,219 to the nearest ten thousand.

4. $837,222 + 768,354 = ?$

5. There are 16 baseball cards in a package. Jill bought 6 packages. How many baseball cards did she buy?

6. Find the median of 11, 9, 22, 16 and 7.

7. $4,000 - 966 = ?$

8. Nine centuries are _____ years.

9. Write the time 20 minutes before noon.

10. $6\dfrac{1}{4} + 8\dfrac{2}{5} = ?$

11. $65 \times 51 = ?$

12. Find the LCM of 12 and 14.

13. The answer to a division problem is the _____.

14. $15,813 \div 7 = ?$

15. How many millimeters are in 5 meters?

16. $62.5 - 36.8 = ?$

17. Find the average of 43, 37, 43, 38 and 39.

18. On the Celsius scale, water freezes at _____.

19. List the factors of 18.

20. Find the perimeter of the rectangle.

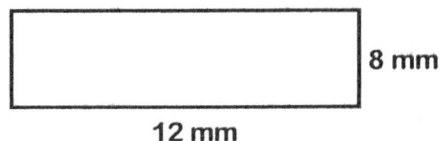

1.	2.	3.	4.
5.	6.	7.	8.
9.	10.	11.	12.
13.	14.	15.	16.
17.	18.	19.	20.

Lesson #45

1. $\dfrac{5}{8} \bigcirc \dfrac{9}{11}$

2. A six-sided polygon is called a(n) _____.

3. Write $3\dfrac{4}{7}$ as an improper fraction.

4. How many degrees are in a straight angle?

5. $4{,}325 \times 6 = ?$

6. Write 14.09 using words.

7. $205 - 78 = ?$

8. Make a factor tree for 32.

9. How many teaspoons are in 8 tablespoons?

10. Put $\dfrac{7}{21}$ in simplest form.

11. $\dfrac{9}{10} - \dfrac{3}{10} = ?$

12. Round 3,209,866 to the nearest hundred.

13. $621 + 588 + 93 = ?$

14. It is 1:15 now. What time was it 7 hours ago?

15. What is the probability of rolling a number greater than 1 on one roll of a die?

16. Are these shapes similar or congruent?

17. $5\dfrac{1}{6} + 3\dfrac{1}{2} = ?$

18. If the diameter of a circle is 18 mm, what is the radius?

19. Write the next number in the sequence. 45, 55, 65, …

20. How many decades are 70 years?

1.

2.

3.

4.

5.

6.

7.

8.

9.

10.

11.

12.

13.

14.

15.

16.

17.

18.

19.

20.

Lesson #46

1. Find the mode of 37, 92, 56, 19 and 56.

2. Write the standard number for $4,000 + 500 + 60 + 9$.

3. $8\frac{1}{9} + 2\frac{1}{3} = ?$

4. Find $\frac{1}{5}$ of 45.

5. Is my house more likely to be 3 inches, 3 feet or 3 miles from the mall?

6. List the factors of 12.

7. How many feet are in 3 miles?

8. The answer to an addition problem is called the _____.

9. $34,816 + 79,065 = ?$

10. Find the volume of the cube.   3 cm

11. $3,478 \bigcirc 3,784$

12. How many pints are in 3 quarts?

13. $57 \times 14 = ?$

14. $836 \div 25 = ?$

15. Find the GCF of 16 and 24.

16. Draw perpendicular lines.

17. Which has more sides a hexagon or a pentagon?

18. What time will it be in 35 minutes, if it is 10:25?

19. Write the first four prime numbers.

20. A closed figure made up of line segments is called a _____.

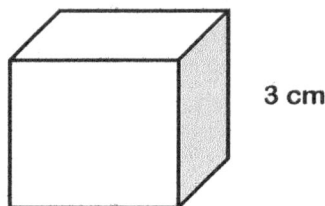

1.

2.

3.

4.

5.

6.

7.

8.

9.

10.

11.

12.

13.

14.

15.

16.

17.

18.

19.

20.

Lesson #47

1. Find the range of 87, 42, 67, 99 and 31.

2. $34 \times 29 = ?$

3. Find the volume of the solid.

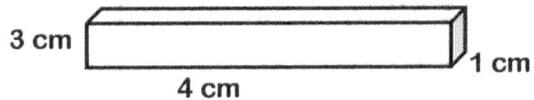

    3 cm | 4 cm | 1 cm

4. List the factors of 16.

5. $286 \div 40 = ?$

6. How many quarts are in 10 gallons?

7. Draw intersecting lines.

8. $\dfrac{2}{3} \bigcirc \dfrac{4}{5}$

9. Write the time 45 minutes after 5:00.

10. Find $\dfrac{1}{3}$ of 27.

11. $18.9 - 9.4 = ?$

12. $10 - 4\dfrac{2}{3} = ?$

13. Which digit is in the hundred thousands place in 6,219,453?

14. Find the perimeter of a pentagon whose sides measure 7 inches each.

15. On a Celsius thermometer, water boils at _____.

16. Find the LCM of 14 and 16.

17. A houseplant would need about 300 ml or 300 L of water at one time?

18. $5\dfrac{1}{5} + 6\dfrac{3}{4} = ?$

19. How many centimeters are 5 meters?

20. $375,816 + 48,932 = ?$

1.	2.	3.	4.
5.	6.	7.	8.
9.	10.	11.	12.
13.	14.	15.	16.
17.	18.	19.	20.

Lesson #48

1. Is the number 19 a prime or a composite number?

2. $80,000 - 39,176 = ?$

3. Find the area of a square whose sides each measure 4 feet.

4. $480 \times 24 = ?$

5. How many cups are in 4 pints?

6. Put $\dfrac{4}{20}$ in simplest form.

7. Draw a line segment.

8. $\dfrac{3}{5} \bigcirc \dfrac{5}{6}$

9. $457 + 386 = ?$

10. Round 4,877,231 to the nearest million.

11. Find $\dfrac{1}{8}$ of 56.

12. What time will it be in 1 hour and 45 minutes, if it is 5:45 now?

13. $148 \div 37 = ?$

14. $\dfrac{3}{10} + \dfrac{2}{5} = ?$

15. Draw a right angle.

16. If the radius of a circle is 12 mm, what is the diameter?

17. $13\dfrac{1}{9} - 10\dfrac{7}{9} = ?$

18. Figures with the same size and shape are _____.

19. How many feet are in 6 yards?

20. Five dozen cookies will be divided evenly among 12 children. How many cookies will each child receive?

1.	2.	3.	4.
5.	6.	7.	8.
9.	10.	11.	12.
13.	14.	15.	16.
17.	18.	19.	20.

Lesson #49

1. Find the GCF of 14 and 21.

2. Draw a hexagon.

3. Find the area of a square whose sides measure 8 centimeters.

4. $35,776 + 48,213 = ?$

5. $\dfrac{4}{5} \bigcirc \dfrac{7}{8}$

6. How many inches are in 4 feet?

7. $6\dfrac{1}{3} + 5\dfrac{2}{5} = ?$

8. $42,066 \div 6 = ?$

9. Round 45,818,296 to the nearest ten thousand.

10. Find $\dfrac{1}{3}$ of 18.

11. Write 'seven and two hundredths' as a decimal.

12. $5,071 - 3,698 = ?$

13. Write $\dfrac{19}{5}$ as a mixed number.

14. Figures with the same shape but different sizes are _____.

15. $8\dfrac{1}{9} - 6\dfrac{7}{9} = ?$

16. Put $\dfrac{15}{25}$ in simplest form.

17. $38,214 \times 4 = ?$

18. Would a coffee table best be weighed in ounces or in pounds?

19. List the factors of 24.

20. How many cups are in 4 pints?

1.	2.	3.	4.
5.	6.	7.	8.
9.	10.	11.	12.
13.	14.	15.	16.
17.	18.	19.	20.

Lesson #50

1. If the diameter of a circle is 10 mm, what is the radius?

2. How many degrees are in a straight angle?

3. Find the volume of this solid figure.

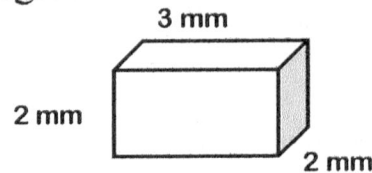

4. Find the LCM of 12 and 16.

5. $4 - 2\dfrac{3}{7} = ?$

6. On a Celsius thermometer, water boils at _____.

7. Make a factor tree for 64.

8. $474 + 398 + 512 = ?$

9. $10\dfrac{2}{3} + 8\dfrac{1}{4} = ?$

10. Find the range of 73, 24, 99 and 18.

11. How many millimeters are in 8 meters?

12. $5,436 \div 6 = ?$

13. $6.2 + 4.9 = ?$

14. Draw a line segment.

15. $\dfrac{5}{9}$ ◯ $\dfrac{7}{10}$

16. $70,000 - 28,453 = ?$

17. Put $\dfrac{8}{24}$ in simplest form.

18. A hexagon has _____ sides.

19. Write $\dfrac{23}{5}$ as a mixed number.

20. Find the perimeter of an octagon whose sides measure 4 cm each.

1.	2.	3.	4.
5.	6.	7.	8.
9.	10.	11.	12.
13.	14.	15.	16.
17.	18.	19.	20.

Lesson #51

1. Susie is 4 feet 5 inches tall. How many inches tall is Susie?

2. Draw an obtuse angle.

3. $473,209 + 886,775 = ?$

4. $16\frac{1}{9} - 12\frac{7}{9} = ?$

5. Write the next number in the sequence. 86, 81, 76, …

6. $350 \div 70 = ?$

7. $39 \times 64 = ?$

8. Write 37,215 in expanded form.

9. How many minutes are in 4 hours?

10. Find the area of a square if one side measures 7 inches.

11. $6,005 - 1,297 = ?$

12. The answer to a division problem is the _____.

13. Find the GCF of 12 and 14.

14. $8\frac{1}{2} + 9\frac{2}{5} = ?$

15. Put $\frac{8}{16}$ in simplest form.

16. Round 7,213,886 to the nearest thousand.

17. How many years are 8 centuries?

18. $\frac{5}{12} \bigcirc \frac{7}{9}$

19. The distance across a circle, through the center, is the _____.

20. If it is 3:40 now, what time was it 4 hours and 10 minutes ago?

1.

2.

3.

4.

5.

6.

7.

8.

9.

10.

11.

12.

13.

14.

15.

16.

17.

18.

19.

20.

Lesson #52

1.   Find the perimeter of a hexagon whose sides measure 4 mm.

2. $432 \times 25 = ?$

3. $5.23 + 8.7 = ?$

4.   List the factors of 18.

5.   Find the median and the mode of 24, 46, 32, 18 and 24.

6. $40,000 - 32,888 = ?$

7.   Draw perpendicular lines.

8.   Write $\dfrac{31}{5}$ as a mixed number.

9.   How many feet are in 7 yards?

10.   Make a factor tree for 56.

11. $8,624 \div 4 = ?$

12.   Write the next number in the sequence. 80, 71, 62, …

13.   There are _____ degrees in a right angle.

14. $\dfrac{8}{9}$ $\bigcirc$ $\dfrac{3}{4}$

15.   Write $4\dfrac{2}{7}$ as an improper fraction.

16.   Is 47 a prime or a composite number?

17. $6\dfrac{1}{8} - 2\dfrac{5}{8} = ?$

18.   Find $\dfrac{1}{5}$ of 50.

19. $4\dfrac{2}{3} + 6\dfrac{1}{5} = ?$

20.   Write the even numbers between 20 and 29.

1.	2.	3.	4.
5.	6.	7.	8.
9.	10.	11.	12.
13.	14.	15.	16.
17.	18.	19.	20.

Lesson #53

1. What will be the time nine minutes before 4:00?

2. $8 - 3\frac{2}{7} = ?$

3. Find the volume of the rectangular solid.

4. Put $\frac{3}{21}$ in simplest form.

5. On a Fahrenheit thermometer, water boils at _____.

6. Write 'fifteen and twenty-one hundredths' as a decimal number.

7. Find the LCM of 9 and 15.

8. $4\frac{1}{7} + 8\frac{1}{3} = ?$

9. What is the probability of rolling an even number on one roll of a die?

10. Would a scooter best be weighed in ounces or in pounds?

11. Find $\frac{1}{6}$ of 36.

12. Draw intersecting lines.

13. Find the area of a rectangle that is 9 in. long and 7 in. wide.

14. Which digit is in the millions place in 36,021,547?

15. How many grams are in 6 kilograms?

16. Find the range of 38, 100, 19 and 45.

17. An eight-sided polygon is a(n) _____.

18. $503 - 199 = ?$

19. $49 \times 25 = ?$

20. Mary is making punch. The recipe calls for 1 gallon of liquid. If she has already added 2 pints and 1 quart, how many more quarts does Mary need to add?

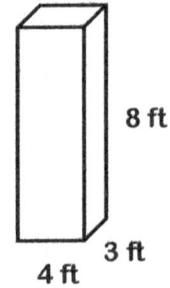

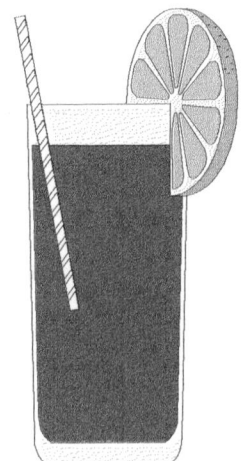

1.	2.	3.	4.
5.	6.	7.	8.
9.	10.	11.	12.
13.	14.	15.	16.
17.	18.	19.	20.

Lesson #54

1. Draw a ray.

2. $364 + 287 = ?$

3. Find the perimeter of a square whose sides measure 3 feet each.

4. How many months are in 3 years?

5. Round 3,263,551 to the nearest hundred.

6. Write the first four prime numbers.

7. $18 - 13\frac{5}{9} = ?$

8. $3,210 - 1,776 = ?$

9. Put $\frac{9}{27}$ in simplest form.

10. What will be the time 40 minutes after 6:00?

11. Is 42 a prime or a composite number?

12. $5\frac{1}{9} + 3\frac{1}{2} = ?$

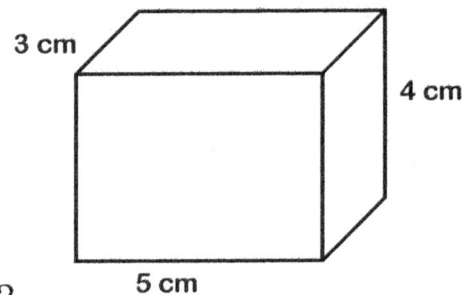

13. Find the volume of this solid figure.

14. How many degrees are in a straight angle?

15. $87 \times 45 = ?$

16. $\frac{4}{11} \bigcirc \frac{5}{6}$

17. How many pounds are in 6 tons?

18. Make a factor tree for 20.

19. Find the median of 30, 19, 22, 16 and 41.

20. Draw a pentagon.

1.	2.	3.	4.
5.	6.	7.	8.
9.	10.	11.	12.
13.	14.	15.	16.
17.	18.	19.	20.

Lesson #55

1. Write 6.08 using words.

2. Find the perimeter of a pentagon if each side measures 8 inches.

3. $14\frac{2}{3} + 9\frac{1}{5} = ?$

4. Round 38,215,077 to the nearest ten thousand.

5. If the diameter of a circle is 12 mm, what is the radius?

6. Find the GCF of 10 and 25.

7. Water freezes at what Celsius temperature?

8. $235 \times 36 = ?$

9. $30,000 - 19,375 = ?$

10. $12\frac{1}{7} - 10\frac{5}{7} = ?$

11. How many feet are in 3 miles?

12. Draw a line of symmetry on the hexagon.

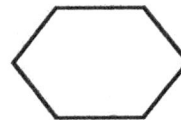

13. Write 44,235 in expanded form.

14. $840 \div 70 = ?$

15. Sharon was 12th in line to buy tickets for an Indians' baseball game. How many people were in front of her?

16. Draw an acute angle.

17. Write $\frac{41}{5}$ as a mixed number.

18. How many centimeters are in 4 meters?

19. $337,218 + 887,993 = ?$

20. List the factors of 12.

1.	2.	3.	4.
5.	6.	7.	8.
9.	10.	11.	12.
13.	14.	15.	16.
17.	18.	19.	20.

Lesson #56

1. $73 + 26 + 17 = ?$

2. In Fahrenheit, water freezes at _____.

3. $13 - 8\dfrac{5}{6} = ?$

4. $388,754 + 662,581 = ?$

5. Round 39,210,568 to the nearest million.

6. Find the area of a square whose sides each measure 9 centimeters.

7. Two figures with the same size and shape are _____.

8. $7,230 - 3,986 = ?$

9. Make a factor tree for 40.

10. $\dfrac{4}{9} \bigcirc \dfrac{3}{7}$

11. How many ounces are in 3 pounds?

12. Draw 2 similar hexagons.

13. $350 \div 50 = ?$

14. The middle number in a set of numbers is the _____.

15. Write $3\dfrac{2}{9}$ as an improper fraction.

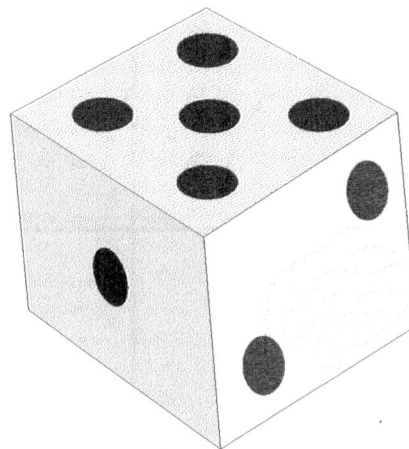

16. $38 \times 23 = ?$

17. Write 25,613 in expanded form.

18. What is the probability of rolling a four on one roll of a die?

19. Write the odd numbers between 32 and 40.

20. How many teaspoons are in 3 tablespoons?

1.	2.	3.	4.
5.	6.	7.	8.
9.	10.	11.	12.
13.	14.	15.	16.
17.	18.	19.	20.

Lesson #57

1.   Write 'nineteen and four tenths' as a decimal.

2.   Draw parallel horizontal lines.

3. $53,218 + 69,774 = ?$

4. $18\frac{1}{7} - 11\frac{6}{7} = ?$

5.   Put $\frac{9}{36}$ in simplest form.

6. $49 \times 51 = ?$

7.   How many pints are in 5 quarts?

8.   The answer to a division problem is called the _____.

9. $\frac{8}{12}$ ◯ $\frac{9}{10}$

10. Round 42,816,755 to the nearest thousand.

11. $5\frac{1}{3} + 9\frac{1}{4} = ?$

12. Find the volume of a rectangular prism with a length of 8 cm, a width of 5 cm and a height of 2 cm.

13. $600 - 299 = ?$

14. On a Fahrenheit thermometer, water boils at _____.

15. Find the range of 86, 73, 28, 42 and 105.

16. $4,550 \div 50 = ?$

17. How many tons are 6,000 pounds?

18. A polygon with four sides is called a(n) _____.

19. Write $7\frac{2}{3}$ as an improper fraction.

20. Find the LCM of 14 and 18.

1.	2.	3.	4.
5.	6.	7.	8.
9.	10.	11.	12.
13.	14.	15.	16.
17.	18.	19.	20.

Lesson #58

1. How many feet are in 5 miles?

2. $\dfrac{5}{8} \times \dfrac{16}{25} = ?$

3. Draw a right angle.

4. Find the perimeter of this rectangle.

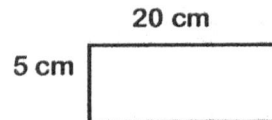

    5 cm, 20 cm

5. $17\dfrac{1}{8} - 9\dfrac{5}{8} = ?$

6. Write 36,215 in expanded form.

7. $66,374 + 98,355 = ?$

8. Round 2,455,919 to the nearest ten thousand.

9. $6\dfrac{2}{5} + 8\dfrac{1}{4} = ?$

10. $720 \div 30 = ?$

11. Danny was 5 feet 2 inches tall. What is his height in inches?

12. $70,000 - 43,552 = ?$

13. Make a factor tree for 32.

14. $331 \times 28 = ?$

15. Find the GCF of 12 and 18.

16. A math book would best be weighed in ounces or in pounds?

17. $2,475 \div 5 = ?$

18. If the radius of a circle is 12 mm, what is the diameter?

19. How many quarts are in 7 gallons?

20. $\dfrac{3}{8} \bigcirc \dfrac{5}{7}$

1.	2.	3.	4.
5.	6.	7.	8.
9.	10.	11.	12.
13.	14.	15.	16.
17.	18.	19.	20.

Lesson #59

1. Are these shapes congruent?

2. $403,575 + 186,691 = ?$

3. $5\dfrac{1}{7} + 3\dfrac{1}{3} = ?$

4. Put $\dfrac{10}{15}$ in simplest form.

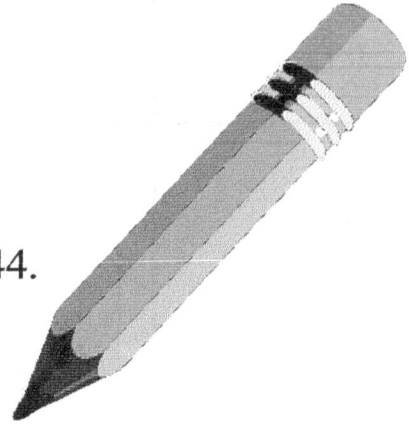

5. James bought a pack of 12 pencils for \$1.44. How much did each pencil cost?

6. How many inches are in 2 yards?

7. $403 - 196 = ?$

8. Find the perimeter of this square.

9. $\dfrac{5}{7} = \dfrac{?}{21}$

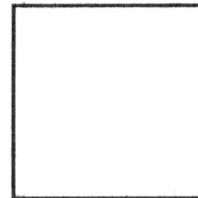

4 ft

10. $318 \times 25 = ?$

11. Round 93,114,587 to the nearest ten thousand.

12. If a play began at 8:15 p.m. and lasted for 1 hour and 45 minutes, at what time did the play end?

ADMIT ONE

13. Find the LCM of 8 and 12.

14. $87,256 \div 6 = ?$

15. Write $\dfrac{53}{9}$ as a mixed number.

16. How many pints are in 4 quarts?

17. $15 - 10\dfrac{3}{5} = ?$

18. Find $\dfrac{1}{9}$ of 36.

19. Draw an obtuse angle.

20. Find the average of 12, 13, 22, 13 and 15.

1.

2.

3.

4.

5.

6.

7.

8.

9.

10.

11.

12.

13.

14.

15.

16.

17.

18.

19.

20.

Lesson #60

1. Make a factor tree for 90.

2. $50,000 - 24,315 = ?$

3. How many decades are 80 years?

4. $4\dfrac{2}{7} + 4\dfrac{1}{5} = ?$

5. Find the area of the quadrilateral.

6. $3,600 \div 40 = ?$

7. Write $3\dfrac{4}{7}$ as an improper fraction.

8. $\dfrac{5}{8} = \dfrac{25}{?}$

9. $16\dfrac{1}{10} - 10\dfrac{7}{10} = ?$

10. $14,819 \times 9 = ?$

11. Find the range of 75, 80, 100, 95 and 82.

12. Is $\dfrac{3}{7}$ in simplest form?

13. $\dfrac{4}{7} \bigcirc \dfrac{5}{8}$

14. Maureen's garden contains 5 rows of plants with 10 plants in each row. How many plants are in her garden?

15. $45,712 + 22,949 = ?$

16. A four-sided polygon is called a(n) _____.

17. Is the width of a paper clip about 1 centimeter or 1 meter?

18. $\dfrac{4}{5} + \dfrac{1}{5} = ?$

19. How many centimeters are 6 meters?

20. In a bag of marbles, four are red and three are green. What is the probability of picking a green one? A red one?

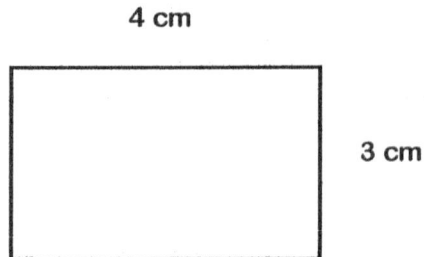

4 cm

3 cm

1.

2.

3.

4.

5.

6.

7.

8.

9.

10.

11.

12.

13.

14.

15.

16.

17.

18.

19.

20.

Lesson #61

1. $8\frac{1}{5} + 3\frac{3}{4} = ?$

2. Is this figure a polygon?

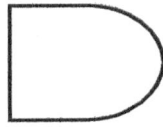

3. $3,007 - 1,689 = ?$

4. Identify this angle by type.

5. $\frac{5}{9} \times \frac{18}{20} = ?$

6. Round 364,531 to the nearest thousand.

7. Write $1\frac{5}{8}$ as an improper fraction.

8. Find the average of 59, 63, 75, 53 and 65.

9. Put $\frac{12}{18}$ in simplest form.

10. $4,863 \times 7 = ?$

11. True or false? A six-sided polygon is called a sixagon.

12. Find the area of a square whose sides each measure 5 inches.

13. $897 \div 38 = ?$

14. How many cups are in 4 pints?

15. $\frac{3}{7} \bigcirc \frac{2}{5}$

16. Find the GCF of 14 and 21.

17. $35.7 + 8.92 = ?$

18. The number that occurs most often in a set of numbers is the _____.

19. $437,806 + 831,215 = ?$

20. Is the sum in problem #19 an even or an odd number?

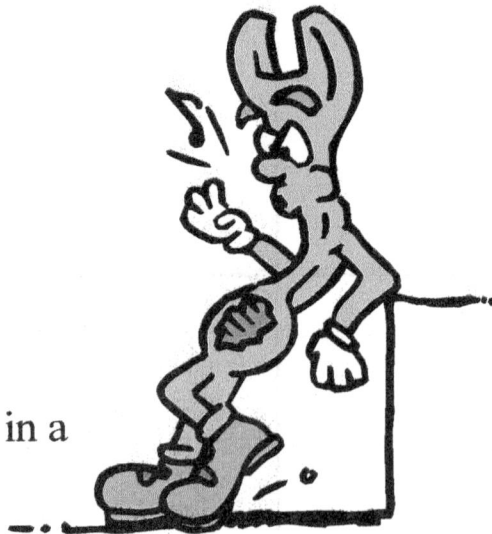

1.

2.

3.

4.

5.

6.

7.

8.

9.

10.

11.

12.

13.

14.

15.

16.

17.

18.

19.

20.

Lesson #62

1. Find the range of 37, 52, 97 and 15.

2. Write $\dfrac{45}{7}$ as a mixed number.

2 ft

3. $35 \times 49 = ?$

4. $4\dfrac{1}{6} - 2\dfrac{5}{6} = ?$

16 ft

5. $8{,}643 \div 3 = ?$

6. Find the area of the rectangle.

7. How many days are in 5 weeks?

8. Find the LCM of 10 and 12.

9. $80{,}000 - 43{,}292 = ?$

10. Which digit is in the hundred thousands place in 5,032,687?

11. Six pints is how many cups?

12. Is the height of a door about 8 feet or 8 yards?

13. $\dfrac{4}{9} = \dfrac{16}{?}$

14. $6\dfrac{1}{9} + 8\dfrac{1}{2} = ?$

15. Find $\dfrac{1}{7}$ of 56.

16. $37{,}414 + 28{,}065 = ?$

17. The answer to a multiplication problem is the _____.

18. What year was it, exactly 6 centuries before 1965?

19. Write 21,463 in expanded form.

20. The Smith family wants to fence their yard. The length of the yard is 96 meters and the width is 52 meters. How much fencing will they need?

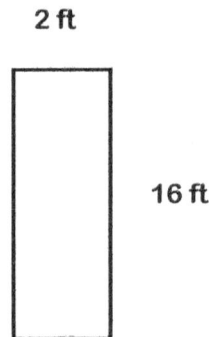

1.

2.

3.

4.

5.

6.

7.

8.

9.

10.

11.

12.

13.

14.

15.

16.

17.

18.

19.

20.

Lesson #63

1. Write $6\dfrac{3}{5}$ as an improper fraction.

2. A pentagon has _____ sides.

3. $307 - 188 = ?$

4. $14\dfrac{2}{7} - 10\dfrac{6}{7} = ?$

5. Write the formula for finding the area of a rectangle.

6. If it is 5:15 now, what time will it be in 8 hours and 10 minutes?

7. $324 \times 23 = ?$

8. The answer to a subtraction problem is called the _____.

9. Draw intersecting lines.

10. What is the probability of rolling a number less than 6 on one roll of a die?

11. If the radius of a circle is 10 mm, what is the circle's diameter?

12. Put $\dfrac{8}{12}$ in simplest form.

13. $9\dfrac{2}{7} + 3\dfrac{1}{4} = ?$

14. List the factors of 10.

15. $\dfrac{4}{5} \times \dfrac{10}{16} = ?$

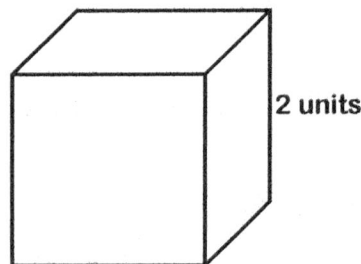

2 units

16. Find the volume of the cube.

17. Draw 2 congruent circles.

18. $2,816 + 14,299 = ?$

19. Make a factor tree for 81.

20. Find the median of 8, 24, 16, 12 and 19.

1.

2.

3.

4.

5.

6.

7.

8.

9.

10.

11.

12.

13.

14.

15.

16.

17.

18.

19.

20.

Lesson #64

1. Find $\dfrac{1}{5}$ of 25.

2. How many yards are in a mile?

3. Draw a right angle.

4. Michael is 6 feet 3 inches tall. What is Michael's height in inches?

5. $\dfrac{4}{9} - \dfrac{2}{9} = ?$

6. The boiling temperature of water, in Fahrenheit, is _____.

7. 4,592 $\bigcirc$ 4,952

8. Write 16.3 using words.

9. $\dfrac{7}{8} \bigcirc \dfrac{9}{10}$

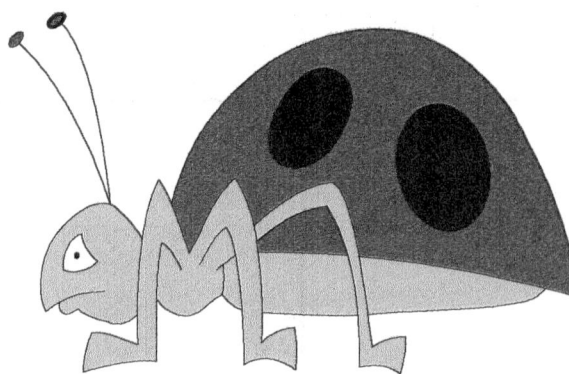

10. $12 - 6\dfrac{4}{5} = ?$

11. Numbers that have only 2 factors are called _____ numbers.

12. What is the perimeter of a regular pentagon whose sides each measure 3 centimeters?

13. $16,346 \div 6 = ?$

14. $263 \times 5 = ?$

15. $10\dfrac{1}{5} - 3\dfrac{3}{4} = ?$

16. How many feet are in 4 yards?

17. $6,031 - 3,446 = ?$

18. $3.7 + 21.9 = ?$

19. A closed figure made up of line segments is a(n) _____.

20. Write the next number in the sequence. 94, 97, 100, …

1.

2.

3.

4.

5.

6.

7.

8.

9.

10.

11.

12.

13.

14.

15.

16.

17.

18.

19.

20.

Lesson #65

1. $13 - 8\frac{3}{8} = ?$

2. How many feet are in 6 yards?

3. A quadrilateral has _____ sides.

4. Put $\frac{12}{18}$ in simplest form.

5. $\frac{3}{8} \times \frac{10}{12} = ?$

6. $361,217 + 487,354 = ?$

7. Write $3\frac{5}{7}$ as an improper fraction.

8. $334 \times 25 = ?$

9. Find the area of a square whose sides measure 3 meters each.

10. $11\frac{2}{5} + 13\frac{1}{4} = ?$

11. Find the GCF of 25 and 30.

12. Draw a line segment.

13. $821 - 375 = ?$

14. How many grams are in 7 kilograms?

15. $\frac{8}{9} \bigcirc \frac{5}{6}$

16. Find the median of 53, 16, 29, 31 and 46.

17. Write 'six and four tenths' as a decimal.

18. Make a factor tree for 60.

19. $480 \div 60 = ?$

20. Round 4,207,334 to the nearest thousand.

1.	2.	3.	4.
5.	6.	7.	8.
9.	10.	11.	12.
13.	14.	15.	16.
17.	18.	19.	20.

Lesson #66

1. $32,406 \times 6 = ?$

2. How many gallons are 8 quarts?

3. $3\dfrac{2}{9} + 5\dfrac{1}{2} = ?$

4. It is 3:40. What time will it be in 6 hours and 20 minutes?

5. $\$63.45 - \$18.99 = ?$

6. Draw a right angle.

7. $43.92 + 18.8 = ?$

8. Put $\dfrac{14}{21}$ in simplest form.

9. Write the next number in the sequence. 32, 39, 46, ...

10. $4,763 \div 3 = ?$

11. The answer to a subtraction problem is called the _____.

12. $\dfrac{4}{7} \times \dfrac{14}{24} = ?$

13. Find the volume of a rectangular prism, if the length is 6 feet, the width is 4 feet and the height is 2 feet.

14. Which digit is in the hundred thousands place in 7,206,345?

15. Find $\dfrac{1}{8}$ of 64.

16. Find the mode of 18, 23, 46, 29 and 23.

17. $\dfrac{4}{7} \bigcirc \dfrac{5}{9}$

18. List the factors of 18.

19. How many feet are in 2 miles?

20. $18\dfrac{1}{6} - 12\dfrac{5}{6} = ?$

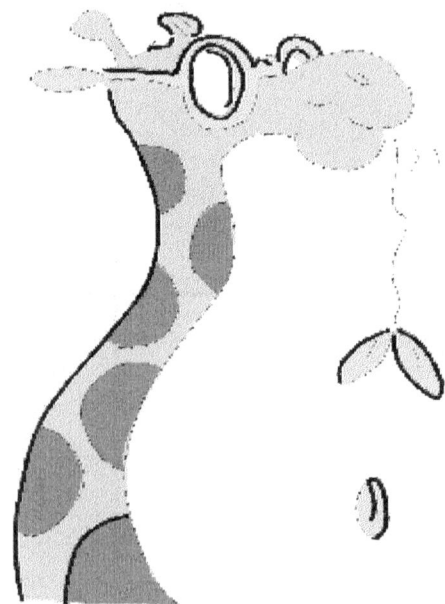

1.

2.

3.

4.

5.

6.

7.

8.

9.

10.

11.

12.

13.

14.

15.

16.

17.

18.

19.

20.

Lesson #67

1.   What type of angle is shown?

2.   How many minutes are in 5 hours?

3.   Write $\dfrac{32}{6}$ as a mixed number.

4.   3,415,291 + 8,229,804 = ?

5.   Which is the greater distance, 6 yards or 6 feet?

6. $2\dfrac{2}{7} + 3\dfrac{1}{4} = ?$

7.   Write 21,235 in expanded form.

8.   On a Celsius thermometer, water boils at what temperature?

9.   Draw intersecting lines.

10. Find the perimeter of a regular hexagon whose sides measure 7 cm.

11. 70,000 − 27,316 = ?

12. 77 × 42 = ?

13. $\dfrac{4}{9} = \dfrac{?}{27}$

14. What time was it 8 hours ago, if it is 2:00 now?

15. Give the name of the figure to the right.

16. How many pounds are 96 ounces?

17. Find the radius of a circle whose diameter is 24 mm.

18. Find the LCM of 12 and 14.

19. 45,235 ÷ 5 = ?

20. Which is heavier 300 grams or 300 kilograms?

1.	2.	3.	4.
5.	6.	7.	8.
9.	10.	11.	12.
13.	14.	15.	16.
17.	18.	19.	20.

Lesson #68

1. Put $\dfrac{12}{16}$ in simplest form.

2. $302 - 176 = ?$

3. Find the volume of a cube whose sides measure 6 inches.

4. Write the first 5 prime numbers.

5. $11\dfrac{1}{2} - 6\dfrac{4}{5} = ?$

6. $86 \times 34 = ?$

7. Make a factor tree for 16.

8. Write the even numbers between 50 and 58.

9. There are _____ degrees in a straight angle.

10. $361{,}247 + 285{,}932 = ?$

11. Write $9\dfrac{2}{3}$ as an improper fraction.

12. Draw a line.

13. Nine centuries are _____ years.

14. Find the average of 135, 375 and 450.

15. Round 86,345,219 to the nearest ten thousand.

16. Numbers with only 2 factors are _____ numbers.

17. $280 \div 41 = ?$

18. Find $\dfrac{1}{5}$ of 35.

19. $8.05 - 0.46 = ?$

20. How many students prefer football over gymnastics?

    Baseball is the favorite sport of how many?

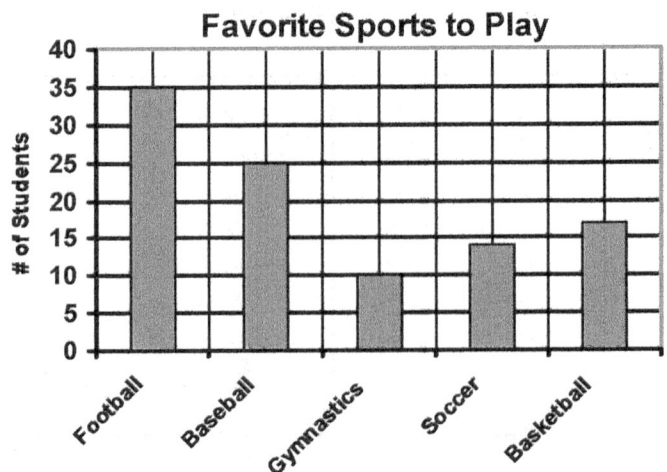

1.	2.	3.	4.
5.	6.	7.	8.
9.	10.	11.	12.
13.	14.	15.	16.
17.	18.	19.	20.

Lesson #69

1. $568,904 + 35,688 = ?$

2.   Draw a hexagon.

3. $245 \times 31 = ?$

4.   Find the perimeter of a pentagon whose sides measure 5 inches.

5.   Find the GCF and the LCM of 12 and 18.

6.   If it is 4:20 now, what time will it be in 7 hours and 15 minutes?

7. $\dfrac{5}{9} \bigcirc \dfrac{7}{8}$

8.   How many inches are in a yard?

9. $\dfrac{6}{7} \times \dfrac{14}{24} = ?$

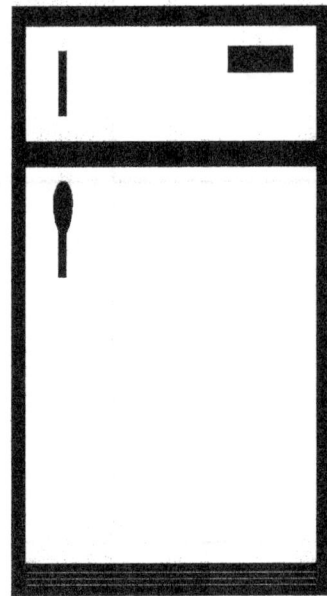

10. $7,023 - 4,889 = ?$

11. $481 \div 14 = ?$

12. Find the range and the median of 34, 88, 92, 13 and 56.

13. How many quarts are in 6 gallons?

14. A refrigerator would best be weighed in pounds or in tons?

15. Round 46,772,098 to the nearest million.

16. $24 - 19\dfrac{7}{8} = ?$

17. Draw an obtuse angle.

18. Figures with the same size and shape are _____.

19. What is the probability of rolling an even number on a single roll of a die?

20. Is 53 a prime or a composite number?

1.	2.	3.	4.
5.	6.	7.	8.
9.	10.	11.	12.
13.	14.	15.	16.
17.	18.	19.	20.

Lesson #70

1. Put $\dfrac{12}{18}$ in simplest form.

2. $45{,}877 \times 3 = ?$

3. How many pounds are 8 tons?

4. Write 'seventy and three hundredths' as a decimal.

5. $50{,}000 - 29{,}444 = ?$

6. Which digit is in the ten thousands place in 679,032?

7. What will be the time 35 minutes after noon?

8. Jason is 6 feet 7 inches tall. How many inches tall is Jason?

9. What is the area of a rectangle whose length is 17 cm and whose width is 4 cm?

10. Draw perpendicular lines.

11. $35.6 - 19.37 = ?$

12. $8\dfrac{1}{3} + 5\dfrac{3}{5} = ?$

13. How many degrees are in a right angle?

14. $678 + 984 + 139 = ?$

15. $45{,}675 \div 5 = ?$

16. How many nickels are in $2?

17. $\dfrac{5}{9} \times \dfrac{12}{15} = ?$

18. The answer to an addition problem is called the _____.

19. Draw two similar pentagons.

20. Find $\dfrac{3}{5}$ of 35.

1.

2.

3.

4.

5.

6.

7.

8.

9.

10.

11.

12.

13.

14.

15.

16.

17.

18.

19.

20.

Lesson #71

1. $67 \times 24 = ?$

2. How many cups are in 4 pints?

3. Write the odd numbers between 50 and 59.

4. Classify the angle by type.

5. $12\frac{1}{6} - 10\frac{5}{6} = ?$

6. The bottom number in a fraction is the _____.

7. From January 1st to June 1st is how many months?

8. Put $\frac{10}{12}$ in simplest form.

9. $314 - 188 = ?$

10. $1\frac{1}{2} \times 2\frac{2}{3} = ?$

11. Write the standard number for $50,000 + 7,000 + 500 + 8$.

12. Karen's ballet class begins at 7:00 p.m. It takes her 10 minutes to walk to the bus stop and 25 minutes for the bus ride. After getting off of the bus, she walks 5 minutes to the class. What time should she leave her house if she wants to get to class on time?

13. $478,903 + 551,266 = ?$

14. $\frac{5}{6} = \frac{25}{?}$

15. $47 + \underline{\quad} = 96$

16. How many millimeters are in 9 meters?

17. Draw a ray.

18. $684 \div 24 = ?$

19. Write 12.46 using words.

20. If the diameter of a circle is 36 inches, what is the radius?

1.

2.

3.

4.

5.

6.

7.

8.

9.

10.

11.

12.

13.

14.

15.

16.

17.

18.

19.

20.

Lesson #72

1. Write $\dfrac{23}{7}$ as a mixed number.

2. $345 \div 25 = ?$

3. Two figures with the same shape but different sizes are _____.

4. $515 - 266 = ?$

5. How many teaspoons are in 9 tablespoons?

6. $89 + 53 + 77 = ?$

7. On the Fahrenheit temperature scale, water freezes at _____.

8. What time was it 4 hours and 5 minutes ago, if it is 1:15 now?

9. Find the LCM of 9 and 15.

10. $\dfrac{7}{9} \bigcirc \dfrac{9}{10}$

11. Find the area of a square if the sides each measure 7 feet.

12. $5\dfrac{2}{5} + 6\dfrac{2}{3} = ?$

13. $9.4 - 6.88 = ?$

14. Find the mode of 44, 67, 29, 91 and 67.

15. Make a factor tree for 64.

16. $93 \times 35 = ?$

17. List the factors of 24.

18. How many degrees are in a straight angle?

19. Which digit is in the thousands place in 348,912?

20. Six hundred years is _____ centuries.

1.	2.	3.	4.
5.	6.	7.	8.
9.	10.	11.	12.
13.	14.	15.	16.
17.	18.	19.	20.

Lesson #73

1. $347 + 625 = ?$

2.   Find the LCM of 12 and 18.

3.   Put $\dfrac{18}{24}$ in simplest form.

4.   Which factors of 14 are also factors of 28?

5. $\dfrac{5}{8} = \dfrac{25}{?}$

6.   Draw 2 similar triangles.

7. $36.7 + 23.4 = ?$

8.   Which digit is in the hundredths place in 42.67?

9.   What is the name of this shape?

10.   Write $\dfrac{12}{5}$ as a mixed number.

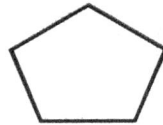

11.   Rename $7\dfrac{3}{4}$ as an improper fraction.

12.   How many inches are in 4 feet?

13. $\dfrac{7}{9} \bigcirc \dfrac{9}{10}$

14. $3\dfrac{1}{3} + 4\dfrac{1}{4} = ?$

15. $\dfrac{15}{20} \times \dfrac{4}{5} = ?$

16. $\dfrac{3}{4} + \dfrac{1}{4} = ?$

17. $\dfrac{6}{10} \div \dfrac{2}{10} = ?$

18.   Would a bike best be weighed in ounces or in pounds?

19. $60 \times 70 = ?$

20.   Give the length of the segment in inches?

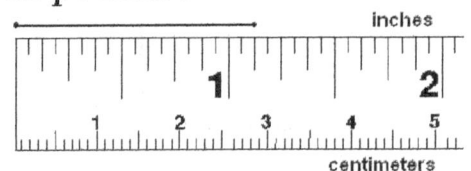

1.	2.	3.	4.
5.	6.	7.	8.
9.	10.	11.	12.
13.	14.	15.	16.
17.	18.	19.	20.

Lesson #74

1.   Draw a line of symmetry in a triangle.

2. $6,000 - 2,347 = ?$

3.   Find the range of 55, 59, 60, 59 and 57.

4.   Find the mode of the set of numbers in problem #3.

5. $53,475 + 27,986 = ?$

6. $775 \times 8 = ?$

7.   Round 36.5 to the nearest whole number.

8. $4.7 \times 2.3 = ?$

9.   What is the area of a rectangle whose length is 15 mm and whose width is 12 mm?

10. $794 \div 5 = ?$

11.   Amy bought 2 videos for $14.00 each, a DVD for $24.99 and a computer game for $37.50. How much change did she get back from a $100 bill?

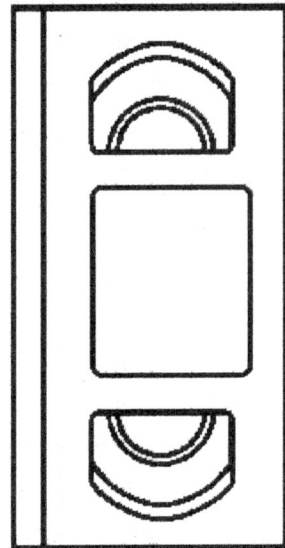

12.   Find the GCF of 10 and 12.

13. $8\dfrac{1}{5} \div 6\dfrac{4}{5} = ?$

14.   How many sides does an octagon have?

15.   Write 16.7 in words.

16.   Rename $\dfrac{15}{4}$ as a mixed number.

17. $\$50.00 - \$36.15 = ?$

18. $8,000 \times 7 = ?$

19.   Find the average of 36, 113, 29, 18 and 54.

20. $\dfrac{6}{7} \bigcirc \dfrac{2}{3}$

1.	2.	3.	4.
5.	6.	7.	8.
9.	10.	11.	12.
13.	14.	15.	16.
17.	18.	19.	20.

Lesson #75

1. $969 \div 8 = ?$

2. Round 18,365 to the nearest thousand.

3. Find the LCM of 8 and 10.

4. $\dfrac{3}{6} = \dfrac{?}{18}$

5. Rename $3\dfrac{1}{3}$ as an improper fraction.

6. $0.08 \times 0.05 = ?$

7. The answer to a division problem is the _____.

8. $1\dfrac{1}{3} \times 2\dfrac{1}{10} = ?$

9. Is 42 a prime or a composite number?

10. $72 \div 8 = ?$

11. List the factors of 36.

12. $\dfrac{12}{15} \times \dfrac{5}{6} = ?$

13. Put $\dfrac{12}{24}$ in simplest form.

14. $5\dfrac{3}{8} - 1\dfrac{5}{12} = ?$

15. In $\dfrac{7}{8}$, which number is in the denominator?

16. How many dimes are in $2?

17. How many milliliters are in a liter?

18. How many centimeters are in 4 meters?

19. On the Celsius scale, water freezes at _____.

20. $(3 \times 6) + 18 = ?$

1.	2.	3.	4.
5.	6.	7.	8.
9.	10.	11.	12.
13.	14.	15.	16.
17.	18.	19.	20.

Lesson #76

1.   On a Fahrenheit thermometer, water freezes at _____.

2. $86 + 24 + 75 = ?$

3. $800 - 655 = ?$

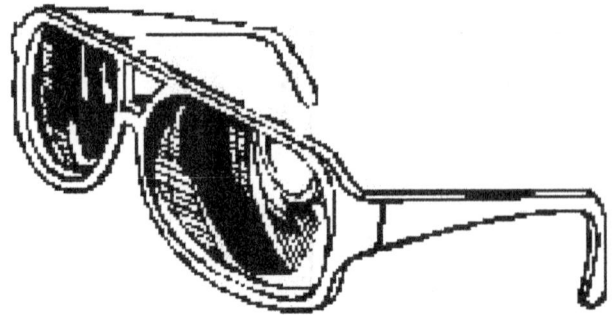

4.   Put $\dfrac{12}{15}$ in simplest form.

5. $2\dfrac{1}{2} + 3\dfrac{1}{3} = ?$

6. $\dfrac{9}{15} \times \dfrac{5}{6} = ?$

7.   Draw a hexagon. How many sides does it have?

8.   Which digit is in the tenths place in 36.75?

9.   Draw intersecting lines.

10. How many pounds are in 4 tons?

11. $5 \times \dfrac{2}{3} = ?$

12. In the morning the temperature was 43°F. By 3:00 p.m. the thermometer read 67°F. What was the change in temperature from morning until afternoon?

13. Find the perimeter of a pentagon if each side measures 6 inches.

14. $65 \times 37 = ?$

15. Find the GCF of 12 and 18.

16. The answer to an addition problem is called the _____.

17. $\dfrac{2}{3} \times \dfrac{9}{12} = ?$

18. Write 65,342 in words.

19. Write the next 3 numbers in the sequence. 57, 64, 71, ...

20. Identify the name of the figure shown to the right.

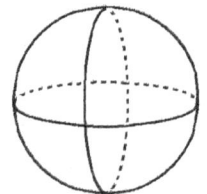

1.	2.	3.	4.
5.	6.	7.	8.
9.	10.	11.	12.
13.	14.	15.	16.
17.	18.	19.	20.

Lesson #77

1. Rename $4\dfrac{2}{3}$ as an improper fraction.

2. Draw intersecting lines.

3. Find the perimeter and the area of a square whose sides measure 12 inches.

4. $45 \times 23 = ?$

5. What is the value of x? $\dfrac{4}{5} = \dfrac{x}{125}$

6. Is the number 21 prime or composite?

7. $652 + 78 + 347 = ?$

8. How many quarters are in $3?

9. $8.3 - 4.75 = ?$

10. Which digit is in the hundredths place in 46.75?

11. How many quarts are in 2 gallons?

12. $\dfrac{2}{6} \times \dfrac{12}{14} = ?$

13. $\dfrac{5}{6} + \dfrac{2}{3} = ?$

14. How many sides does a pentagon have?

15. $\dfrac{7}{8} \bigcirc \dfrac{5}{6}$

16. Find the LCM of 2, 6 and 8.

17. $15,302 - 9,475 = ?$

18. It is 4:20. What time will it be in 3 hours and 10 minutes?

19. Marcus has 3 quarters, 2 dimes and a nickel. How much money does Marcus have?

20. Mario is 4 feet 7 inches tall. What is his height in inches?

1.	2.	3.	4.
5.	6.	7.	8.
9.	10.	11.	12.
13.	14.	15.	16.
17.	18.	19.	20.

Lesson #78

1. Draw an acute angle.

2. $5\dfrac{2}{3} + 6\dfrac{1}{5} = ?$

3. $8.25 + 3.4 = ?$

4. The figure shown is a parallelogram. Draw one.

5. Closed shapes made up of line segments are _____.

6. List the next 3 numbers in the sequence.
    1,100   1,200   1,300   …

7. $1,000 - 467 = ?$

8. $(60 + 5) \div 5 = ?$

9. Draw parallel vertical lines.

10. How many months are there between
    December 1st and May 1st?

11. List the factors of 36.

12. Round 576 to the nearest ten.

13. $436 \times 7 = ?$

14. Draw a rectangle. Label the length 10 cm. and the
    width 7 cm. Find the area of the rectangle.

15. $\dfrac{8}{12} \times \dfrac{6}{16} = ?$

16. $3,175 \div 5 = ?$

17. $7\dfrac{1}{10} + 3\dfrac{3}{10} = ?$

18. What year is 2 decades before 1945?

19. $5\dfrac{1}{4} - 3\dfrac{3}{4} = ?$

20. Give the length of the rectangle in millimeters?

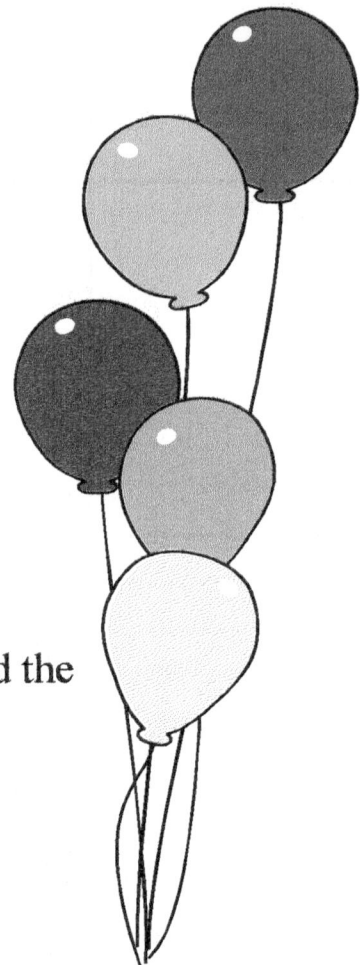

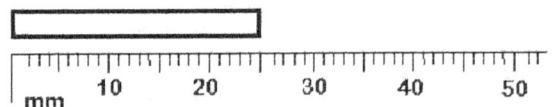

1.	2.	3.	4.
5.	6.	7.	8.
9.	10.	11.	12.
13.	14.	15.	16.
17.	18.	19.	20.

Lesson #79

1. How many ounces are in 5 pounds?

2. Round 5,362 to the nearest thousand.

3. Write the standard number for 'thirty-six and fifteen hundredths.'

4. $36 + 25 + 14 + 51 = ?$

5. $60,000 - 36,478 = ?$

6. Heather read a 324-page book in 4 days. What was the average number of pages she read per day?

7. Find $\dfrac{1}{6}$ of 42.

8. $92 \times 47 = ?$

9. $3,480 \div 40 = ?$

10. $3 - 2\dfrac{1}{2} = ?$

11. Change $\dfrac{7}{2}$ to a mixed number.

12. Change $8\dfrac{3}{4}$ to an improper fraction.

13. Write the next three numbers in the sequence. 61, 56, 51, …

14. If a truck can carry $2\dfrac{1}{2}$ tons, how many pounds can it carry?

15. A puppy weighed $\dfrac{1}{2}$ of a pound. How many ounces did it weigh?

16. $\dfrac{3}{4} = \dfrac{?}{16}$

17. Put $\dfrac{10}{25}$ in simplest form.

18. $3.6 + 2.5 + 1.2 = ?$

19. Write the name of this shape.

20. $6\dfrac{1}{4} + 3\dfrac{2}{5} = ?$

1.	2.	3.	4.
5.	6.	7.	8.
9.	10.	11.	12.
13.	14.	15.	16.
17.	18.	19.	20.

Lesson #80

1. Draw a line segment.

2. $625 \times 3 = ?$

3. How many feet are in 2 miles?

4. $8,020 - 2,765 = ?$

5. List the factors of 18.

6. How many cups are in a pint?

7. $\dfrac{3}{4} \times \dfrac{6}{18} = ?$

8. How many milliliters are in a liter?

9. List the first 5 prime numbers.

10. $\dfrac{7}{8} + \dfrac{1}{8} = ?$

11. $4\dfrac{2}{5} - 2\dfrac{4}{5} = ?$

12. Find $\dfrac{2}{3}$ of 120.

13. $8,652 \div 45 = ?$

14. $\dfrac{3}{7} \bigcirc \dfrac{9}{10}$

15. Find the GCF of 10 and 25.

16. Find the LCM of 10 and 25.

17. Put $\dfrac{9}{12}$ in simplest form.

18. Draw a square. Show 2 lines of symmetry.

19. Are these figures similar or congruent?

20. What fraction is shaded?

1.

2.

3.

4.

5.

6.

7.

8.

9.

10.

11.

12.

13.

14.

15.

16.

17.

18.

19.

20.

Lesson #81

1.   Draw an obtuse angle.

2.   The diameter of a circle is 16 mm. What is its radius?

3. $6.2 \times 0.7 = ?$

4. $3.5 \div 5 = ?$

5.   Is 29 a prime or a composite number?

6. $862 + 479 = ?$

7. $6\dfrac{1}{3} - 3\dfrac{2}{3} = ?$

8.   Find the average and the median of 18, 25, 15, 29 and 18.

9. $70{,}000 - 34{,}973 = ?$

10. $28.8 \div 0.6 = ?$

11.   For each item, would a milliliter or a liter be the more reasonable unit of measure? a) aquarium   b) soup can   c) eye dropper

12. $\dfrac{9}{11} \; \bigcirc \; \dfrac{7}{12}$

13.   Round 5,276,362 to the nearest million.

14.   At a kennel, the ratio of dogs to cats was 4 to 9. If there were 64 dogs, how many cats were at the kennel?

15.   Find the LCM of 9 and 21.

16.   Put these numbers in order from least to greatest.
     3,652   3,498   3,562   3,948

17.   Rename $4\dfrac{1}{2}$ as an improper fraction.

18. $2\dfrac{2}{3} \times 3\dfrac{1}{4} = ?$

19.   At what temperature does water boil in Fahrenheit?

20.   How many inches are in 7 feet?

1.	2.	3.	4.
5.	6.	7.	8.
9.	10.	11.	12.
13.	14.	15.	16.
17.	18.	19.	20.

Lesson #82

1. $6\frac{2}{3} \times 3\frac{1}{5} = ?$

2. How many quarts are in 6 gallons?

3. Find the GCF of 18 and 24.

4. How many dimes are in $3?

5. $8,463 + 24,592 = ?$

6. $36 \times 14 = ?$

7. $\frac{4}{5} \bigcirc \frac{11}{12}$

8. $63 + ? = 97$

9. How many days are in 12 weeks?

10. The radius of a circle is 14 cm. What is circle's diameter?

11. Find the perimeter and the area of a rectangle with a length of 10 yards and a width of 6 yards.

12. Find the median of 48, 72, 83, 49 and 16.

13. Write $\frac{91}{9}$ as a mixed number.

14. Identify this shape by name.

15. Draw a pentagon. Draw a line of symmetry.

16. Figures with the same shape, but different sizes are _____.

17. $580 \div 32 = ?$

18. $10\frac{1}{5} - 3\frac{3}{10} = ?$

19. Find the average of 139, 275, 398 and 420.

20. What is the probability that the spinner will land in the area marked A?

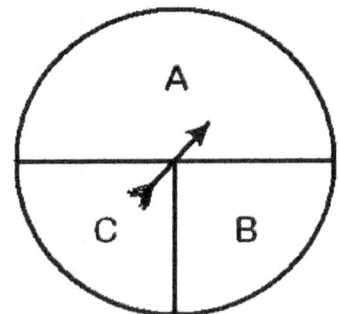

1.	2.	3.	4.
5.	6.	7.	8.
9.	10.	11.	12.
13.	14.	15.	16.
17.	18.	19.	20.

Lesson #83

1. Solve the proportion to find x. $\dfrac{4}{7} = \dfrac{56}{x}$

2. $62.5 + 37.82 = ?$

3. Rename $\dfrac{37}{6}$ as a mixed number.

4. Round 6,575 to the nearest hundred.

5. $5\dfrac{2}{5} \times \dfrac{5}{9} = ?$

6. How many cups are in 4 pints?

7. $6.2 \times 4.1 = ?$

8. Is 17 a prime or a composite number?

9. Find the LCM of 15 and 25.

10. On the Celsius temperature scale, water boils at _____.

11. How many centimeters are in 5 meters?

12. Find the median of 12, 89, 16, 28 and 76.

13. $0.09 \times 0.5 = ?$

14. Find the volume of the prism.   3 cm

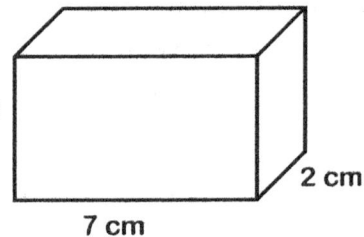

15. $(50 \times 6) \times 2 = ?$

     2 cm

     7 cm

16. Draw a right angle.

17. Write 40% as a fraction in simplest form.

18. $9,860 \div 4 = ?$

19. $4\dfrac{5}{8} - 2\dfrac{1}{4} = ?$

20. What is the probability that the spinner will stop on each?

    a) the number 2
    b) an odd number
    c) a number less than 5

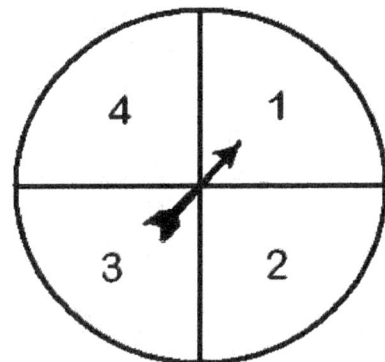

1.

2.

3.

4.

5.

6.

7.

8.

9.

10.

11.

12.

13.

14.

15.

16.

17.

18.

19.

20.

Lesson #84

1. Draw a hexagon. How many sides does it have?

2. $345 + 68 + 9 = ?$

3. $405 \times 16 = ?$

4. $3.4 - 1.72 = ?$

5. $\dfrac{2}{3} + \dfrac{5}{6} = ?$

6. Put $\dfrac{15}{20}$ in simplest form.

7. Find the LCM of 6, 9 and 10.

8. $\dfrac{7}{9} \bigcirc \dfrac{2}{5}$

9. $402 - 176 = ?$

10. How many nickels are in $1?

11. If it is 12:25 now, what time was it 3 hours and 10 minutes ago?

12. Jeff is 6 feet 2 inches tall. How many inches tall is Jeff?

13. Round 23,472 to the nearest thousand.

14. Write 7.2 using words.

15. How many centuries are 900 years?

16. Find the volume of a rectangular prism with a length of 9 inches, a width of 4 inches and a height of 2 inches.

17. How many pounds are in 6 tons?

18. On a Celsius thermometer, water freezes at_____.

19. The diameter of a circle is 18 centimeters. What is the radius?

20. Find the median of 86, 24, 13, 73 and 57.

1.	2.	3.	4.
5.	6.	7.	8.
9.	10.	11.	12.
13.	14.	15.	16.
17.	18.	19.	20.

Lesson #85

1. What is the value of x? $\dfrac{3}{8} = \dfrac{x}{80}$

2. $863 + 479 = ?$

3. Find the average of 42, 90 and 87.

4. An arena has 121 seats arranged in 11 rows, with the same number of seats in each row. How many seats are in each row?

5. $3.2 \times 4.7 = ?$

6. $5.25 \div 3 = ?$

7. Find the GCF of 6 and 10.

8. $\dfrac{1}{4} + \dfrac{2}{5} = ?$

9. $5\dfrac{1}{3} - 2\dfrac{2}{3} = ?$

10. $2.772 \div 2.1 = ?$

11. What is the volume of a rectangular prism whose length is 18 cm, whose width is 16 cm and whose height is 4 cm?

12. $\dfrac{3}{6} \times \dfrac{2}{9} = ?$

13. $\dfrac{3}{7} = \dfrac{?}{21}$

14. Which is the greater volume, 60 milliliters or 40 liters?

15. Write 76.34 using words.

16. Sharon worked $3\dfrac{3}{4}$ hours on Tuesday and $6\dfrac{1}{2}$ hours on Wednesday. How many hours did she work in all?

17. Find the mode of 36, 24, 17, 36 and 54.

18. Find the median of the numbers in problem # 17.

19. Round 36,756,213 to the nearest ten million.

20. How many feet are in a mile?

1.	2.	3.	4.
5.	6.	7.	8.
9.	10.	11.	12.
13.	14.	15.	16.
17.	18.	19.	20.

Lesson #86

1. $56.2 \times 0.06 = ?$

2. How many years are 5 decades?

3. Draw an obtuse angle.

4. $7.6 - 2.75 = ?$

5. Draw an octagon. Label a side 7 inches long. Find the perimeter.

6. Find the GCF and the LCM of 12 and 14.

7. Which digit is in the thousandths place in 32.076?

8. Figures with the same shape and the same size are called?

9. Put $\dfrac{12}{14}$ in simplest form.

10. $1,862 + 9,754 = ?$

11. $5\dfrac{1}{2} + 3\dfrac{1}{4} = ?$

12. How many ounces are in a pound?

13. Round 4,675,213 to the nearest ten thousand.

14. $60,000 - 39,417 = ?$

15. $4.35 \div 0.5 = ?$

16. In Fahrenheit, water boils at _____.

17. Write $\dfrac{47}{5}$ as a mixed number.

18. $\dfrac{3}{4} \div \dfrac{1}{2} = ?$

19. $4\dfrac{2}{5} - 2\dfrac{4}{5} = ?$

20. Use the pie graph to answer the following:

    a) What percent of students got an A in math?

    b) What percent got a B in math?

    c) What percent got a C or a D in math?

Student Math Grades

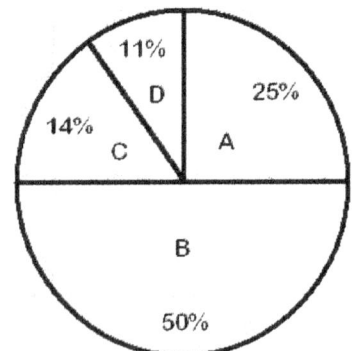

11%
D   25%
14%   A
C
B
50%

1.	2.	3.	4.
5.	6.	7.	8.
9.	10.	11.	12.
13.	14.	15.	16.
17.	18.	19.	20.

Lesson #87

1. $\dfrac{3}{8} \times \dfrac{12}{15} = ?$

2. How many centimeters are in 9 meters?

3. $6.75 \div 0.5 = ?$

4. $7\dfrac{1}{5} - 3\dfrac{3}{5} = ?$

5. Find the LCM of 10 and 15.

6. $\dfrac{6}{7} \bigcirc \dfrac{5}{6}$

7. Is 81 a prime or a composite number?

8. List the next 3 numbers in the sequence. 58, 64, 70, …

9. Find the area of a rectangle that is 12 feet long and 6 feet wide.

10. $8\dfrac{1}{2} + 6\dfrac{3}{4} = ?$

11. The ratio of girls to boys at the park is $\dfrac{5}{6}$. If there are 35 girls, how many boys are at the park?

12. The diameter of a circle is 14 in. What is the radius?

13. Change $3\dfrac{1}{3}$ to an improper fraction.

14. How many pounds are in $4\dfrac{1}{2}$ tons?

15. $63 \times 47 = ?$

16. List the factors of 24.

17. Draw a parallelogram.

18. Mike bought a 12-pack of Cola for $3.99, a bag of chips for $2.89 and a candy bar for $0.59. What was his change from a $10 bill?

19. What fraction is shaded?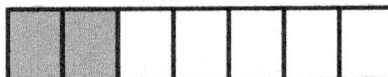

20. Round 8,762 to the nearest ten.

1.	2.	3.	4.
5.	6.	7.	8.
9.	10.	11.	12.
13.	14.	15.	16.
17.	18.	19.	20.

Lesson #88

1.   Matt ate 3 oranges today. If he eats 14 oranges in a week, what fraction of the week's oranges did he eat today?

2. $\dfrac{5}{6} \times \dfrac{12}{15} = ?$

3. $\dfrac{3}{5} + \dfrac{2}{5} = ?$

4.   Draw intersecting lines.

5.   Write 67.25 in words.

6. $365 + 476 + 213 = ?$

7.   Round 56.47 to the nearest whole number.

8. $800 - 154 = ?$

9. $3\dfrac{1}{6} - 2\dfrac{5}{6} = ?$

10.   Draw a ray.

11.   How many inches are in a yard?

12.   A quadrilateral has _____ sides.

13.   Would a pencil best be weighed in ounces or in pounds?

14.   A six-sided shape is a(n) _____.

15. $6.2 + 4.75 = ?$

16.   List the factors of 18.

17. $5\dfrac{2}{3} + 3\dfrac{1}{6} = ?$

18. $4.73 - 2.965 = ?$

19.   Put these decimals in order from least to greatest.
      4.62   4.6   4.0   4.623

20.   Write $\dfrac{15}{4}$ as a mixed number.

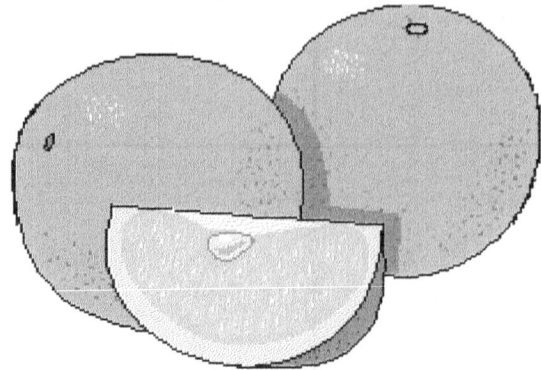

1.

2.

3.

4.

5.

6.

7.

8.

9.

10.

11.

12.

13.

14.

15.

16.

17.

18.

19.

20.

Lesson #89

1. $5.2 - 3.64 = ?$

2.   Draw 2 similar rectangles.

3.   Which digit is in the tenths place in 39.47?

4.   Put these decimals in order from greatest to least.
      2.07   2.007   2.0   2.70

5. $573 \times 9 = ?$

6.   Put $\dfrac{14}{16}$ in simplest form.

7.   Write $6\dfrac{2}{5}$ as an improper fraction.

8. $782 + 463 + 219 = ?$

9.   How many days are in 6 weeks?

10.   Find the perimeter and the area of a square if a side measures 10 ft.

11. $\dfrac{5}{6} = \dfrac{?}{36}$

12. $7,000 - 2,643 = ?$

13.   Find the GCF of 16 and 24.

14.   It is 12:35. What time was it 3 hours and 35 minutes ago?

15.   Find $\dfrac{2}{5}$ of 20.

16.   List the factors of 12.

17.   Sharice ran 550 yards in 3 minutes. At this rate, how many yards can she run in 6 minutes?

18. $1,200 \div 38 = ?$

19.   What part is shaded? Write your answer as a decimal and as a fraction.

20. $3 \times \dfrac{5}{6} = ?$

1.

2.

3.

4.

5.

6.

7.

8.

9.

10.

11.

12.

13.

14.

15.

16.

17.

18.

19.

20.

Lesson #90

1. $182 \times 15 = ?$

2.   Solve the proportion for x. $\dfrac{4}{5} = \dfrac{x}{75}$

3.   Draw a line segment.

4. $4\dfrac{2}{7} - 2\dfrac{5}{7} = ?$

5. $\dfrac{8}{16} \times \dfrac{12}{14} = ?$

6. $5.1 - 3.72 = ?$

7. $\dfrac{5}{6} \bigcirc \dfrac{2}{3}$

8. $\dfrac{4}{10} \div \dfrac{2}{10} = ?$

9.   Would a semi-truck best be weighed in tons or in pounds?

10.   Find the volume of the rectangular prism.

11.   Write the number 56.897 in words.

12. $76,908 + 34,775 = ?$

13. $(400 + 500) + 300 = ?$

5 in

14.   Find the value of x. $\dfrac{3}{10} = \dfrac{x}{100}$

3 in

15. $5,090 - 2,765 = ?$

6 in

16. $16.8 \times 1.2 = ?$

Student Hair Color

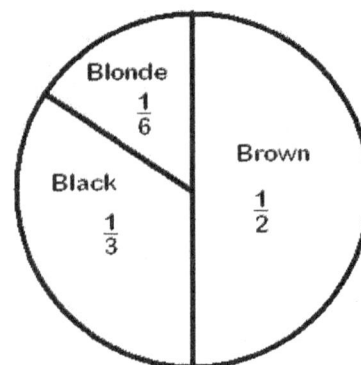

17. $9.52 \div 0.28 = ?$

18. $1\dfrac{2}{3} \div \dfrac{7}{8} = ?$

Blonde $\frac{1}{6}$

Brown $\frac{1}{2}$

Black $\frac{1}{3}$

19.   There are 30 students in the class. How many have blonde hair?

20.   How many have black hair?

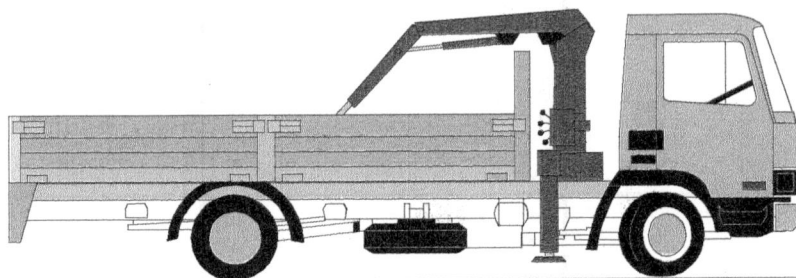

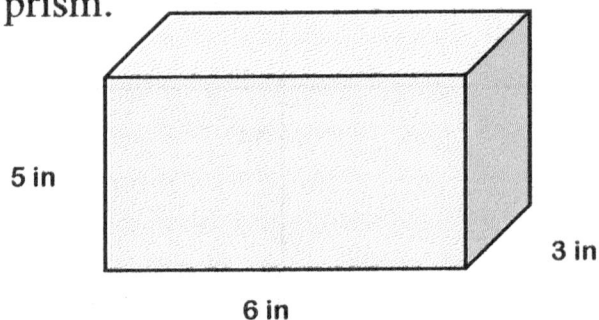

1.

2.

3.

4.

5.

6.

7.

8.

9.

10.

11.

12.

13.

14.

15.

16.

17.

18.

19.

20.

Lesson #91

1.   Round $45.67 to the nearest dollar.

2.   What time will it be in 8 hours and 15 minutes if it is 12:30 now?

3. $52.92 \div 2.1 = ?$

4. $45 + 89 + 135 = ?$

5. $3 \times 5 \times 7 \times 2 = ?$

6.   Find the area of a rectangle whose length is 15 meters and whose width is 10 meters.

7. $4.56 - 1.3 = ?$

8.   Find the value of x. $\dfrac{3}{8} = \dfrac{x}{120}$

9. $20,000 - 12,703 = ?$

10. Round 3,782,906 to the nearest hundred thousand.

11. Write the standard number for 'sixteen and thirty-six hundredths.'

12. $\dfrac{3}{2} \div \dfrac{2}{3} = ?$

13. $5\dfrac{1}{7} + 7\dfrac{2}{3} = ?$

14. Write $\dfrac{17}{3}$ as a mixed number.

15. $\dfrac{12}{18} \times \dfrac{9}{10} = ?$

16. Find the LCM of 15 and 25.

17. Give the name for this type of shape.

18. $3\dfrac{1}{5} - 1\dfrac{4}{5} = ?$

19. The radius of a circle is 8 mm, what is the diameter?

20. What is the length of the base of the triangle?

1.	2.	3.	4.
5.	6.	7.	8.
9.	10.	11.	12.
13.	14.	15.	16.
17.	18.	19.	20.

Lesson #92

1. $4,000 \div 16 = ?$

2.   Find $\dfrac{1}{7}$ of 56.

3. $\dfrac{2}{3} \div \dfrac{1}{4} = ?$

4. $359 + 981 = ?$

5.   How many ounces are in 5 pounds?

6. $0.735 \times 0.5 = ?$

7. $4.3 - 1.21 = ?$

8.   Find the GCF of 8 and 24.

9. $\dfrac{2}{3} - \dfrac{1}{6} = ?$

10.   If $\dfrac{2}{5}$ of the class was absent, what fraction was present?

11.   Find the perimeter of a square whose sides measure 12 yards each.

12.   Find the average of 78, 84 and 87.

13.   How many centimeters are in 7 meters?

14.   Which digit is in the ten thousands place in the number 624,798?

15.   Is the number in problem #14 even or odd?

16.   Solve for x: $\dfrac{2}{5} = \dfrac{x}{15}$

17.   Put $\dfrac{10}{12}$ in simplest form.

18. $\$100 - \$88.74 = ?$

19.   List the factors of 24.

20. $5 - 1\dfrac{2}{5} = ?$

1.	2.	3.	4.
5.	6.	7.	8.
9.	10.	11.	12.
13.	14.	15.	16.
17.	18.	19.	20.

Lesson #93

1. Round 34.89 to the nearest tenth.

2. Write the standard number for 'six and fourteen hundredths.'

3. $40,000 - 24,786 = ?$

4. $4\dfrac{1}{4} - 2\dfrac{3}{4} = ?$

5. $3.67 \times 0.5 = ?$

6. Draw a pentagon. Show a line of symmetry.

7. $208.4 \div 8 = ?$

8. The Thomas family spent $4.95 each for 2 adult movie tickets and $3.50 each for 3 children's tickets. They spent $17.98 on snacks and $4.50 on parking. How much did the Thomas family spend?

9. $1\dfrac{4}{9} + 3\dfrac{2}{3} = ?$

10. Which factors of 20 are also factors of 45?

11. Draw perpendicular lines.

12. Put the decimals in order from least to greatest.
    3.7   3.07   3.77   3.077

13. Eight weeks are how many days?

14. $897 + 653 = ?$

15. $4 \times \dfrac{2}{3} = ?$

16. It is 3:10. What time will it be in 6 hours and 5 minutes?

17. Solve for x: $\dfrac{4}{5} = \dfrac{x}{65}$

18. How many dimes are in 6 dollars?

19. Find the mode of these numbers:
    45, 89, 67, 89, 23 and 50.

20. What part is shaded? Write your answer as a decimal and as a fraction.

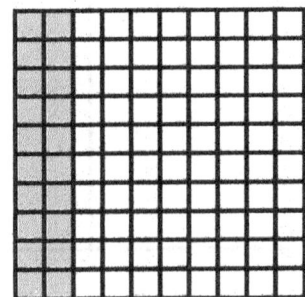

1.	2.	3.	4.
5.	6.	7.	8.
9.	10.	11.	12.
13.	14.	15.	16.
17.	18.	19.	20.

Lesson #94

1. How many minutes are in 6 hours?

2. $2.5 \times 3.6 = ?$

3. The heart of a basset hound pumps 10.4 liters of blood in 5 minutes. How many liters of blood per minute is this?

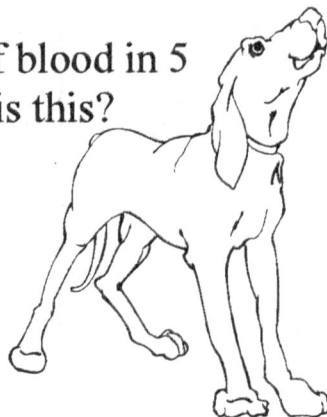

4. Make a factor tree for 32.

5. $6 - 2\frac{7}{8} = ?$

6. $468 + 988 = ?$

7. Draw a right angle. How many degrees are in a right angle?

8. Write 56.79 in words.

9. Round 4,875,908 to the nearest ten thousand.

10. A paper clip would best be weighed in grams or in kilograms?

11. How many centimeters are in 9 meters?

12. $\frac{4}{5} \bigcirc \frac{2}{3}$

13. $\frac{4}{5} + \frac{7}{8} = ?$

14. Find the perimeter and the area of a rectangle whose length is 12 ft. and whose width is 5 ft.

15. On the Celsius temperature scale, water freezes at _____.

16. $56.78 + 9.34 = ?$

17. How many pounds are 80 ounces?

18. Write 45% as a decimal and a reduced fraction.

19. Find the perimeter of this irregular shape.

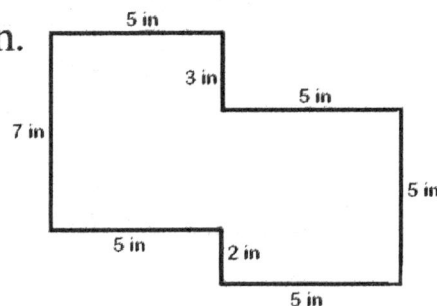

20. What is the average of 84, 86, 92, 95 and 98?

1.	2.	3.	4.
5.	6.	7.	8.
9.	10.	11.	12.
13.	14.	15.	16.
17.	18.	19.	20.

Lesson #95

1. What is the sixth prime number?

2. $3,975,442 + 5,799,523 = ?$

3. Find the product of 0.56 and 2.4.

4. How many pounds are $4\frac{1}{2}$ tons?

5. Find $\frac{3}{5}$ of 45.

6. $18,000 - 6,988 = ?$

7. Figures that have the same shape and the same size are _____.

8. Which digit is in the thousandths place in 334.887?

9. Draw a ray.

10. Find the GCF and LCM of 16 and 20.

11. $5\frac{1}{7} - 3\frac{5}{7} = ?$

12. Which is greater, 0.78 or 0.708?

13. $\frac{5}{6} \times \frac{12}{15} = ?$

14. Write 0.36 as a percent and as a reduced fraction.

15. $35.6 + 98.67 = ?$

16. $(50 \times 5) \div 25 = ?$

17. $\frac{5}{9} \bigcirc \frac{7}{10}$

18. Find the mode of the numbers 50, 37, 88, 50 and 67.

19. What temperature is shown on the thermometer?

20. Water freezes at 32°F. The temperature on this thermometer is how many degrees above freezing?

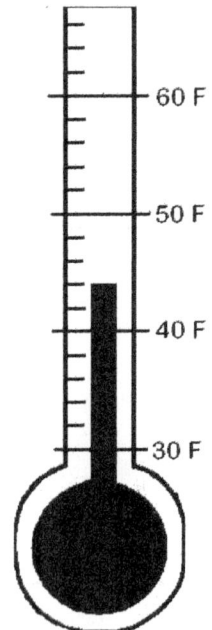

1.

2.

3.

4.

5.

6.

7.

8.

9.

10.

11.

12.

13.

14.

15.

16.

17.

18.

19.

20.

1. The Adams family's yard is 22 meters long and 12 meters wide. If they want to fence in their yard, how much fencing will they need?

2. How many pounds are 400 ounces?

3. $45.8 \times 2.6 = ?$

4. $54.08 \div 0.4 = ?$

5. $6 - 2\dfrac{2}{3} = ?$

6. How many seconds are in 4 hours?

7. Make a factor tree for 36.

8. $\dfrac{4}{5} + \dfrac{7}{8} = ?$

9. Find the area of a square if a side measures 15 millimeters?

10. Solve to find the value of x. $\dfrac{8}{9} = \dfrac{120}{x}$

11. What is the answer to a multiplication problem called?

12. What is the fifth number in the sequence? 32, 38, 44, ...

13. What time was it 3 hours and 15 minutes ago, if it is 5:20 now?

14. How many milliliters are in 4 liters?

15. $\dfrac{5}{11} \div \dfrac{15}{22} = ?$

16. Write the number 356,997 in expanded notation.

17. Find the median of 13, 78, 56, 44 and 21.

18. Write $6\dfrac{5}{10}$ as a decimal.

19. Ten of thirty students received an A on the Science test. What fraction of the students received an A on the test?

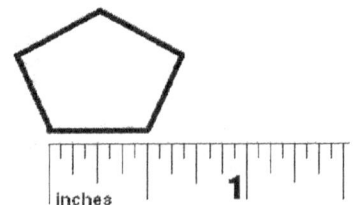

20. How long, in inches, is the base of the pentagon?

1.

2.

3.

4.

5.

6.

7.

8.

9.

10.

11.

12.

13.

14.

15.

16.

17.

18.

19.

20.

Lesson #97

1.   One hour and ten minutes is how many seconds?

2.   How many feet are in 4 miles?

3.   Write the name of this shape.

4. $45.79 - 23.6 = ?$

5.   List the factors of 20.

6. $4\dfrac{5}{6} + 3\dfrac{2}{3} = ?$

7.   How many inches are in 6 yards?

8.   On the Celsius scale, water freezes at what temperature?

9.   Find $\dfrac{2}{7}$ of 21.

10. What is the value of x? $\dfrac{5}{9} = \dfrac{x}{135}$

11. $3,070 - 1,224 = ?$

12. The distance across a circle is called the diameter. What do we call the distance around the outside of a circle?

13. Write $\dfrac{4}{5}$ as a decimal and as a percent.

14. The radius of a circle is 50 cm. What is the diameter?

15. Rename $\dfrac{8}{6}$ as a mixed number.

16. $997 \div 53 = ?$

17. Draw two similar triangles.

18. $15 - 8\dfrac{1}{6} = ?$

19. Is the angle obtuse or acute?

20. What is the probability that the above spinner will stop on an even number? On an odd number? On a number less than 4?

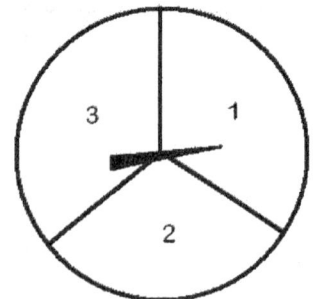

1.

2.

3.

4.

5.

6.

7.

8.

9.

10.

11.

12.

13.

14.

15.

16.

17.

18.

19.

20.

Lesson #98

1. $342 \times 25 = ?$

2. On the 1st day of practice Tom did 3 sit-ups. The next day, he did 5. On the 3rd day he did 8, and on the 4th day, 12 sit-ups. If this pattern continues, how many sit-ups will he do on the 6th day?

3. Find the volume of the rectangular prism to the right.

    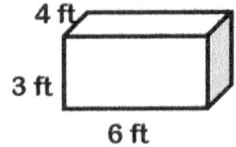

4. $28,897 \div 9 = ?$

5. Name each polygon. a) ◯ b) ⬠ c) ⬡

6. $7 - 3\frac{1}{3} = ?$

7. Write 0.45 as a percent and as a reduced fraction.

8. $\frac{3}{8} \bigcirc \frac{5}{6}$

9. Write 104.87 in words.

10. The ratio of oranges to apples is 5 to 6. If there are 84 apples, how many oranges are there?

11. Round 4,776,223 to the nearest hundred thousand.

12. $\frac{5}{6} \times \frac{10}{15} = ?$

13. A ball weighs 2 pounds, 3 ounces. What is the weight in ounces?

14. How many inches are in 2 yards?

15. $\frac{12}{2} \div \frac{1}{2} = ?$

16. Put $\frac{12}{20}$ in simplest form.

17. Lynn needs $130 to buy a coat. She has $45. If she saves $5 each week, in how many weeks will she have enough to buy the coat?

18. How many nickels are in $6?

19. $456 + 26 + 998 = ?$

20. Solve the proportion for x. $\frac{2}{7} = \frac{x}{91}$

1.	2.	3.	4.
5.	6.	7.	8.
9.	10.	11.	12.
13.	14.	15.	16.
17.	18.	19.	20.

Lesson #99

1. $4\frac{1}{3} - 1\frac{2}{3} = ?$

2. Bill bought 7 pounds of cherries for \$3.43. What was the price for a pound of cherries?

3. Mary's height is 5 feet 2 inches. How many inches tall is Mary?

4. $37.6 + 9.8 + 23.45 = ?$

5. What fraction is shaded?

6. How many yards are in one half of a mile?

7. Which digit is in the tenths place in 245.786?

8. Order these decimals from least to greatest.
    3.08   3.8   3.008   3.0

9. What is $\frac{3}{4}$ of 16?

10. $14.58 \div 0.6 = ?$

11. How many faces does a cube have?

12. Estimate the product of 632 and 470 by rounding to the nearest hundred.

13. $\frac{4}{5} \times \frac{15}{16} = ?$

14. Write $\frac{3}{25}$ as a decimal and as a percent.

15. The radius of a circle is 8 inches. What is the diameter?

16. Put $\frac{8}{10}$ in simplest form.

17. What is the shape of a can of peas?

18. $\frac{15}{6} \div \frac{5}{6} = ?$

    6 yd

    3

    3

19. Find the volume of this rectangular prism.

20. The perimeter of a square is 24 inches. How long is each side?

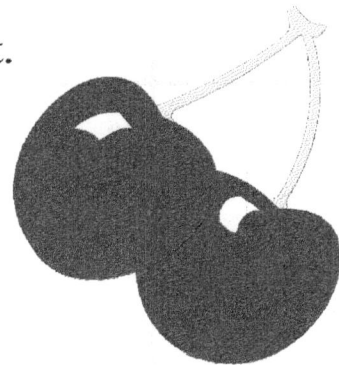

1.	2.	3.	4.
5.	6.	7.	8.
9.	10.	11.	12.
13.	14.	15.	16.
17.	18.	19.	20.

Lesson #100

1. $5,091 - 1,677 = ?$

2. $(400 + 300) - 250 = ?$

3. $3.1 \times 2.3 = ?$

4. $\dfrac{3}{5} \times \dfrac{5}{9} = ?$

5. Write 65% as a decimal and as a reduced fraction.

6. Manuel can run 660 yards in 3 minutes. At this rate, how many yards could he run in 9 minutes?

7. $\dfrac{6}{7} + 2\dfrac{1}{14} = ?$

8. Solve for x. $\dfrac{3}{5} = \dfrac{x}{75}$

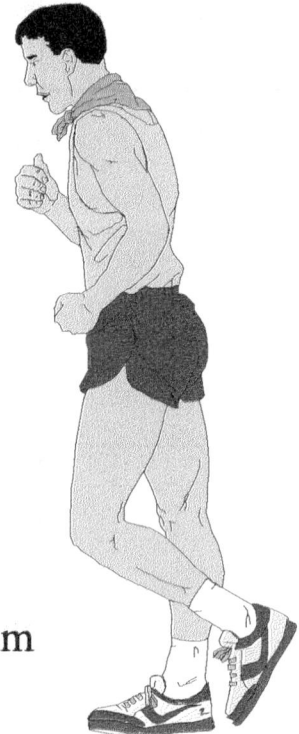

9. Find the GCF and LCM of 10 and 15.

10. Make a factor tree for 64.

11. Round $7.54 to the nearest dollar.

12. $2.6 + 9.87 + 5.1 = ?$

13. How many cups are in 4 pints?

14. Find the area of a rectangle whose length is 11 mm and whose width is 6 mm.

15. How many teaspoons are in 3 tablespoons?

16. Nate worked on his homework from 3:30 p.m. to 5:00 p.m. For how many minutes did he work on his homework?

17. $3\dfrac{5}{8} + 1\dfrac{7}{8} = ?$

18. A six-sided shape is a(n) _____.

19. The answer to a subtraction problem is the _____.

20. $0.300 \div 4 = ?$

1.

2.

3.

4.

5.

6.

7.

8.

9.

10.

11.

12.

13.

14.

15.

16.

17.

18.

19.

20.

Lesson #101

1. $356 + 982 = ?$

2.   Find $\dfrac{1}{6}$ of 42.

3.   How many days are in 2 years?

4. $3\dfrac{4}{5} + 2\dfrac{1}{4} = ?$

5.   Round 23,788,665 to the nearest million.

6.   Draw a rectangle. Show two lines of symmetry.

7. $45.6 - 9.87 = ?$

8. $\dfrac{4}{7} \times \dfrac{14}{16} = ?$

9.   Which is greater, 0.65 or 0.065?

10. Is 19 a prime or a composite number?

11. Find the area of a square whose sides measure 14 millimeters.

12. How many feet are in 3 miles?

13. Write $3\dfrac{7}{10}$ as a decimal.

14. $\dfrac{9}{10} \bigcirc \dfrac{8}{9}$

15. Estimate the product of 89 and 32.

16. The area of a square is 100 cm^2. What is the measure of each side?

17. $\dfrac{5}{6} \div \dfrac{5}{2} = ?$

18. Which digit is in the hundredths place in 24.67?

19. Which factors of 18 are also factors of 24?

20. The answer to a division problem is called the _____.

1.

2.

3.

4.

5.

6.

7.

8.

9.

10.

11.

12.

13.

14.

15.

16.

17.

18.

19.

20.

Lesson #102

1. $56.7 - 25.34 = ?$

2. $1.2 \div 0.12 = ?$

3. How many yards are in a mile?

4. Round 24,786,098 to the nearest thousand.

5. Find the average of 68, 72, 68, 76 and 76.

6. Find $\dfrac{1}{3}$ of 27.

7. $\dfrac{4}{5} \times \dfrac{15}{16} = ?$

8. $5\dfrac{8}{9} + 4\dfrac{4}{9} = ?$

9. Write the standard number for $7{,}000 + 500 + 80 + 9$.

10. Write the decimal number for 'fifteen and three hundredths.'

11. Harry is 6 feet 4 inches tall. How many inches tall is Harry?

12. Find the LCM of 12 and 18.

13. $2\dfrac{1}{4} \div 4\dfrac{1}{2} = ?$

14. Arrange these decimals in order from greatest to least.
    0.3   0.31   0.301

15. $\dfrac{5}{7} \bigcirc \dfrac{9}{11}$

16. Find the area of the parallelogram.

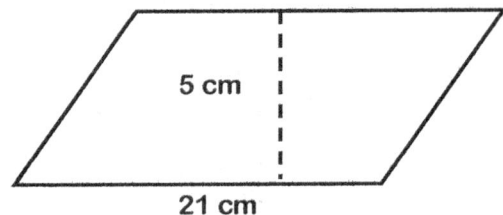

    5 cm

    21 cm

17. A triangle with two congruent sides is a(n) _____ triangle.

18. $346 + 899 = ?$

19. On a Fahrenheit thermometer, water boils at _____.

20. How many inches are in 3 yards?

1.

2.

3.

4.

5.

6.

7.

8.

9.

10.

11.

12.

13.

14.

15.

16.

17.

18.

19.

20.

Lesson #103

1. A triangle with all sides congruent is a(n) _____ triangle.

2. Write $\dfrac{3}{5}$ as a decimal and as a percent.

3. $432 \div 30 = ?$

4. Find the circumference of a circle whose diameter is 15 meters.

5. $\dfrac{6}{7} \times \dfrac{14}{20} = ?$

6. Find the median of 34, 88, 76, 45 and 33.

7. Which digit is in the hundredths place in 9.07?

8. Estimate the product of 497 and 322.

9. The area of a square is 144 mm^2. What is the length of each side?

10. In a class of 30 students $\dfrac{2}{5}$ are boys. How many students are boys?

11. Find the area of a circle whose radius is 6 inches. (A= πr^2)

12. If it is 5:30 now, what time will it be in 4 hours and 15 minutes?

13. How many centimeters are in 7 meters?

14. List the factors of 18.

15. Find the volume of this rectangular prism.

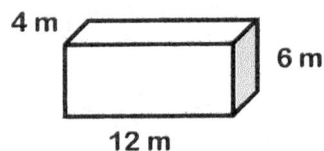

16. $2,000 - 799 = ?$

17. A straight angle has how many degrees?

18. How many years are in 8 centuries?

19. $0.67 \times 1.5 = ?$

20. Use the graph to answer the questions.

    a. Name the shape located at (3,2)

    b. Name the shape located at (4,3)

    c. Give the pair of numbers that locates the hexagon.

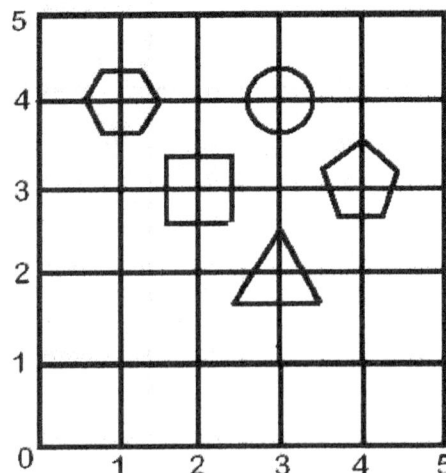

1.

2.

3.

4.

5.

6.

7.

8.

9.

10.

11.

12.

13.

14.

15.

16.

17.

18.

19.

20.

Lesson #104

1. A parallelogram with a 12 ft. base and 7 ft. high has what area?

2. $246,998 + 655,287 = ?$

3. Find $\dfrac{1}{5}$ of 35.

4. $3\dfrac{1}{4} - 1\dfrac{5}{8} = ?$

5. Make a factor tree for 81.

6. Round 246.87 to the nearest tenth.

7. Solve for x. $\dfrac{7}{8} = \dfrac{x}{120}$

8. How many ounces are in 8 pounds?

9. The answer to a multiplication problem is the _____.

10. Find the perimeter of the rectangle on the right.

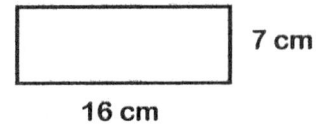

11. Draw a ray.

12. A five-sided shape is called a(n) _____.

13. Find the value of x. $\dfrac{5}{6} = \dfrac{x}{36}$

14. Which factors of 12 are also factors of 18?

15. A piece of paper would best be weighed in ounces or in pounds?

16. Write $\dfrac{14}{5}$ as a mixed number.

17. On the Celsius temperature scale, water boils at _____.

18. $234 \times 121 = ?$

19. Rob is in school 6 hours each day. What fraction of the day is Rob in school?

20. Which letter names the point (1, 4)?

    Which letter names the point (4, 3)?

    Which pair of numbers locates pt. D?

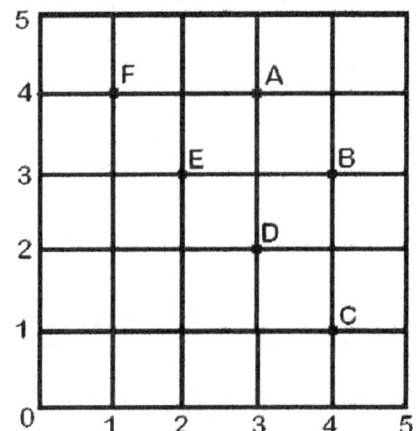

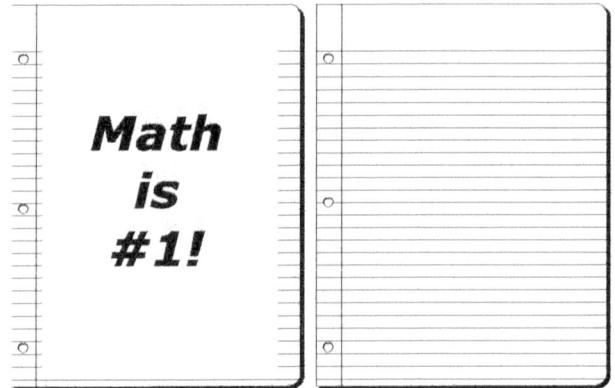

1.

2.

3.

4.

5.

6.

7.

8.

9.

10.

11.

12.

13.

14.

15.

16.

17.

18.

19.

20.

Lesson #105

1. Draw perpendicular lines.

2. Find $\frac{2}{5}$ of 20.

3. $34.56 + 89.9 = ?$

4. $7 - 3\frac{2}{3} = ?$

5. Triangles with no congruent sides are called _____.

6. How many years are in 7 decades?

7. $4.5 \times 6.7 = ?$

8. $\frac{8}{9} \times \frac{9}{14} = ?$

9. Write 0.16 as a percent and as a reduced fraction.

10. $2,907 - 893 = ?$

11. Find the value of x. $\frac{5}{6} = \frac{x}{90}$

12. The area of a square is 64 ft^2. What is the length of each side?

13. How many teaspoons are in 2 tablespoons?

14. It is 2:00 now. What time was it 8 hours ago?

15. The largest cake ever baked was made from 31,026 boxes of cake mix. If each box of cake mix called for 2 eggs, how many <u>dozen</u> eggs were used to make the cake?

16. $83.7 \div 0.9 = ?$

17. Find the LCM of 9 and 15.

18. Draw a line segment.

19. Would the diameter of a ring best be measured in millimeters or kilometers?

20. The radius of a circle is 15 feet. What is the diameter?

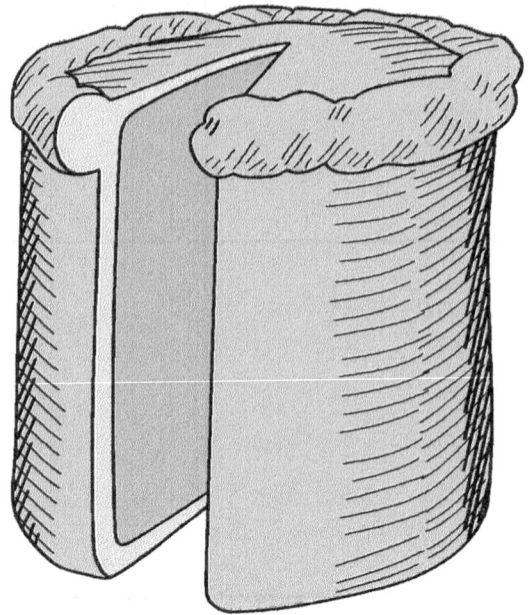

1.	2.	3.	4.
5.	6.	7.	8.
9.	10.	11.	12.
13.	14.	15.	16.
17.	18.	19.	20.

Lesson #106

1. $47 \times 86 = ?$

2.   Round 35,688,900 to the nearest thousand.

3.   Solve the proportion for x. $\dfrac{2}{9} = \dfrac{x}{81}$

4. $709.8 \div 0.6 = ?$

5.   On a Fahrenheit thermometer, water freezes at _____.

6.   The thickness of a penny would best be measured in millimeters or in meters?

7.   Fourteen liters is how many milliliters?

8.   Find the circumference of a circle whose diameter is 8 feet.

9.   Find $\dfrac{2}{3}$ of 15.

10.   Find the area of a parallelogram if its base is 10 inches and it is 4 inches high.

11. $346,887 + 665,219 = ?$

12.   Which digit is in the tenths place in 2.78?

13.   List the first four prime numbers.

14   Find the mode of 23, 67, 99, 67 and 43.

Find the ordered pair for each building.

15.   Hotel _____

16.   Food Store _____

17.   Bank _____

18.   Restaurant _____

19.   Train Station _____

20.   Post Office _____

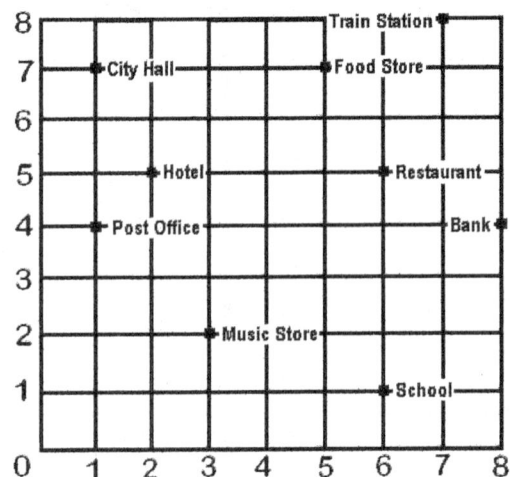

1.

2.

3.

4.

5.

6.

7.

8.

9.

10.

11.

12.

13.

14.

15.

16.

17.

18.

19.

20.

Lesson #107

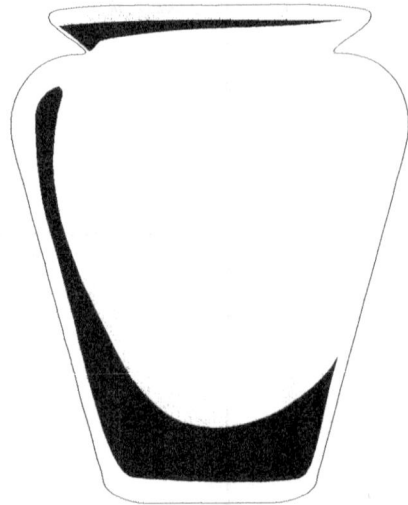

1. Write 34.56 in words.

2. How many yards are in a mile?

3. $4\frac{1}{3} - 2\frac{2}{3} = ?$

4. $\frac{5}{6} + \frac{2}{3} = ?$

5. Write 467,899 in expanded notation.

6. $78.9 - 12.76 = ?$

7. Which is greater, 0.78 or 0.782?

8. $\frac{4}{5} \bigcirc \frac{8}{10}$

9. List the factors of 24.

10. A triangle with no congruent sides is _____.

11. What is the distance around the outside of a circle called?

12. Put $\frac{6}{12}$ in simplest form.

13. What do you call a four-sided polygon?

14. $600 - 98 = ?$

15. Find the volume of the rectangular prism.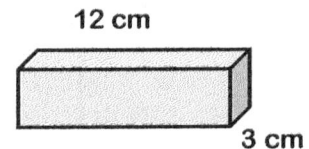

16. How many days are in 9 weeks?

17. An art class has taken orders for 300 ceramic vases. If they can make 15 vases in a day, how long will it take to fill the order?

18. Is the number 19 a prime or a composite number?

19. Which digit is in the hundred thousands place in 2,566,975?

20. Write a decimal for the part that is shaded.

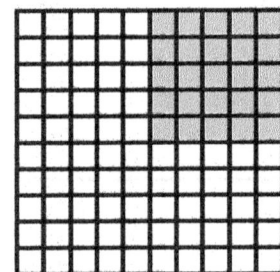

1.	2.	3.	4.
5.	6.	7.	8.
9.	10.	11.	12.
13.	14.	15.	16.
17.	18.	19.	20.

Lesson #108

1. $89.67 + 45.6 = ?$

2. How many ounces are in 3 pounds?

3. $30,000 - 18,439 = ?$

4. $4\frac{5}{6} + 3\frac{2}{3} = ?$

5. Find the average of 18, 42, 17, 31, 7 and 23.

6. $6.8 \times 1.7 = ?$

7. Find the area of a square if a side measures 16 centimeters.

8. Find the GCF of 10 and 25.

9. The length of a fishing pole is probably 5 feet or 5 miles?

10. Any number multiplied by zero has an answer of _____.

11. An isosceles triangle has _____ congruent sides.

12. Write 42% as a decimal and as a reduced fraction.

13. How many feet are in 4 miles?

14. $\frac{7}{8} - \frac{3}{4} = ?$

15. $\frac{5}{8} \div \frac{3}{8} = ?$

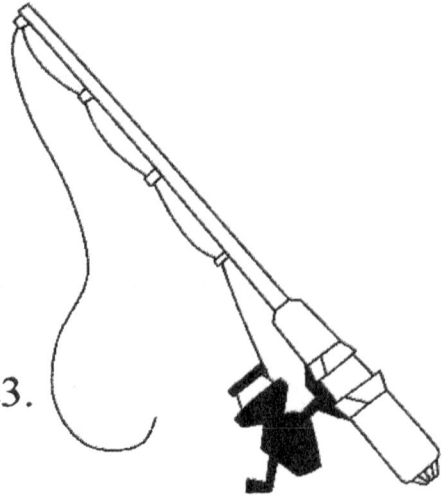

16. Sixty people make up the cast of a local play. 25 are men, 20 are women and 15 are children. What fraction of the cast are children?

17. A polygon with six sides is a _____.

18. Estimate the difference of 567 and 235.

19. Find the value of x. $\frac{5}{8} = \frac{x}{96}$

20. Draw a straight angle. How many degrees are in a straight angle?

1.	2.	3.	4.
5.	6.	7.	8.
9.	10.	11.	12.
13.	14.	15.	16.
17.	18.	19.	20.

Lesson #109

1. How many centimeters are in 8 meters?

2. Find the area and the perimeter of a square if a side is 15 cm long.

3. $3.2 \times 0.4 = ?$

4. $\dfrac{5}{6} - \dfrac{2}{3} = ?$

5. Draw an acute angle.

6. Find the LCM of 15 and 25.

7. $40,000 - 26,788 = ?$

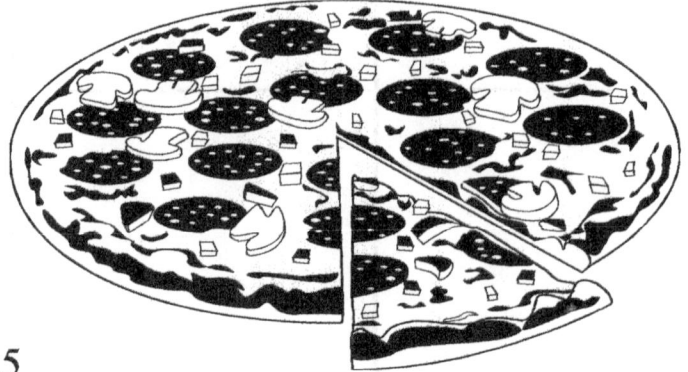

8. What is the value of x? $\dfrac{3}{5} = \dfrac{15}{x}$

9. Write the ratio 'four to seven' in two other ways.

10. The California Cougars, a team of 40 players, ate 20 pizzas after their game. How many pizzas would be needed for 120 players?

11. $62 + 19 + 247 = ?$

12. $5 - 2\dfrac{3}{5} = ?$

13. How many quarts are in 6 gallons?

14. Write 0.7623 in words.

15. $55.55 \div 0.05 = ?$

16. $\dfrac{5}{12} \times \dfrac{1}{5} = ?$

17. Find $\dfrac{2}{3}$ of 12.

18. Write $\dfrac{10}{3}$ as a mixed number.

19. Reduce $\dfrac{9}{12}$ to simplest terms.

20. Jeff had 60 cookies. How many cookies did he have left, if he gave $\dfrac{2}{5}$ of them to Mike and $\dfrac{1}{5}$ of them to Peter?

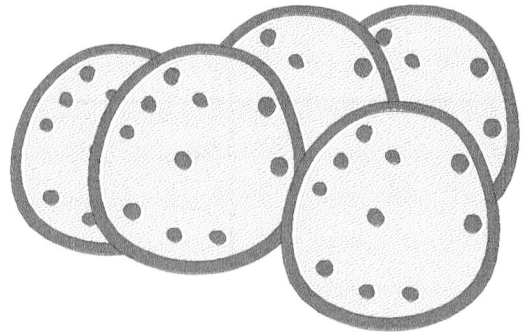

1.	2.	3.	4.
5.	6.	7.	8.
9.	10.	11.	12.
13.	14.	15.	16.
17.	18.	19.	20.

Lesson #110

1. Find the mode of 32, 37, 32, 35 and 36.

2. What is the median of the set of numbers in problem #1?

3. $1,053 \div 27 = ?$

4. A five-sided shape is a(n) _____.

5. $5,516 \times 7 = ?$

6. Round 36,786,514 to the nearest hundred thousand.

7. Jerry spent \$52.50 for a new jacket, \$69.99 for new shoes and \$12 for a new tie. How much did he spend?

8. Find the value of x. $\dfrac{2}{64} = \dfrac{4}{x}$

9. $3,652 + 45,896 = ?$

10. Write the ratio $\dfrac{5}{7}$ in another way.

11. Put $\dfrac{12}{15}$ in simplest form.

12. $0.6 - 0.275 = ?$

13. $54 \div 5 = ?$

14. How many degrees make up a straight angle?

15. $0.004 \times 0.07 = ?$

16. Find $\dfrac{2}{5}$ of 40.

17. Is 13 a prime or a composite number?

18. Put these decimals in order from least to greatest.
    0.1   0.02   0.356   0.035

19. $0.816 \div 6.8 = ?$

20. List the factors of 24.

1.

2.

3.

4.

5.

6.

7.

8.

9.

10.

11.

12.

13.

14.

15.

16.

17.

18.

19.

20.

Lesson #111

1. Write $4\dfrac{5}{8}$ as an improper fraction.

2. Which factors of 16 are also factors of 24?

3. $4\dfrac{3}{4}+2\dfrac{3}{8}=?$

4. $35 \times 43 = ?$

5. Would the most reasonable unit of measurement for the length of a paintbrush be centimeters or meters?

6. Find the volume of a rectangular prism with a length of 12 inches, a width of 4 inches and a height of 3 inches.

7. $\dfrac{4}{5}-\dfrac{1}{4}=?$

8. $\dfrac{3}{8}\times\dfrac{12}{15}=?$

9. Draw 2 congruent rectangles.

10. $5\dfrac{1}{5}-2\dfrac{4}{5}=?$

11. The temperature at 9:00 a.m. was 35°F. At 3:00 p.m., it was 15° warmer, but by 9:00 pm. it fell by 25°. What was the temperature at 9:00 p.m.?

12. $1.4 \times 1.4 = ?$

13. Are the ratios $\dfrac{3}{5}$ and $\dfrac{9}{15}$ equivalent?

14. $3.069 \div 3.3 = ?$

15. The diameter of a circle is 18 cm. What is the radius?

16. If 5 yards of lace can make a dress, how many yards of lace are needed to make 15 dresses?

17. Find the average of 310, 421 and 424.

18. Closed figures made up of line segments are _____.

19. If $3x = 15$, what is the value of x?

20. Is this a slide, a rotation or a reflection? ⬅ ➡

1.	2.	3.	4.
5.	6.	7.	8.
9.	10.	11.	12.
13.	14.	15.	16.
17.	18.	19.	20.

Lesson #112

1. How many years are in 9 decades?

2. Find the GCF of 14 and 21.

3. Find the LCM of 14 and 21.

4. $34.8 + 9.7 + 16.77 = ?$

5. Write 4.753 in words.

6. Round 24,887,663 to the nearest ten thousand.

7. $60,000 - 45,777 = ?$

8. Round 34.876 to the nearest hundredth.

9. Write the ratio 16:18 in another way and put it in simplest form.

10. Solve the proportion for a. $\dfrac{9}{15} = \dfrac{a}{10}$

11. What time was it 6 hours and 5 minutes ago, if it is 3:15 now?

12. Find $\dfrac{3}{5}$ of 25.

13. Find the area of a rectangle that is 14 m long and 6 m wide.

14. How many sides does each polygon have?
    a) hexagon   b) pentagon   c) quadrilateral

15. Dave drove 2 miles on Tuesday, 4 miles on Wednesday, 8 miles on Thursday, and 16 miles on Friday. If this pattern continues (including the weekend), how far will Dave drive by Monday?

16. $2\dfrac{1}{2} \times 3\dfrac{1}{10} = ?$

17. $\dfrac{6}{10} \div \dfrac{3}{10} = ?$

18. Figures with the same shape, but different sizes are _____.

19. $\dfrac{5}{9} \bigcirc \dfrac{4}{7}$

20. Find the perimeter of a square whose sides each measure 13 feet.

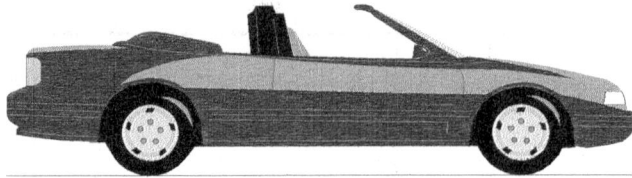

1.	2.	3.	4.
5.	6.	7.	8.
9.	10.	11.	12.
13.	14.	15.	16.
17.	18.	19.	20.

Lesson #113

1. $2\frac{1}{6} \times 3\frac{1}{3} = ?$

2. $4,579 + 32,886 = ?$

3. How many years are in 7 centuries?

4. Find the LCM of 12 and 20.

5. $\frac{4}{10} \div \frac{2}{10} = ?$

6. Write $\frac{34}{5}$ as a mixed number.

7. Write 8.4573 in words.

8. Round 34.87 to the nearest tenth.

9. $50,000 - 29,555 = ?$

10. How many inches are in 4 yards?

11. What is the value of x? $\frac{x}{35} = \frac{3}{7}$

12. Make a factor tree for 42.

13. The ratio of soups to salads is eleven to five. Write this ratio in two other ways.

14. Find the area of a square if a side measures 7 feet.

15. Draw a right angle. How many degrees are in a right angle?

16. The radius of a circle is 22 inches. What is the diameter?

17. $64 \times 35 = ?$

18. $\frac{2}{3} \bigcirc \frac{5}{6}$

19. $\frac{3}{4} + \frac{7}{8} = ?$

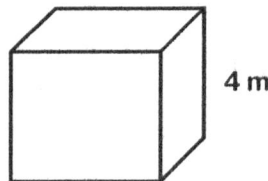

4 m

20. Find the volume of this cube.

1.

2.

3.

4.

5.

6.

7.

8.

9.

10.

11.

12.

13.

14.

15.

16.

17.

18.

19.

20.

Lesson #114

1. $1.45 \times 0.03 = ?$

2. Put these decimals in order from greatest to least.
    3.46   3.046   3.326   3.406

3. $11\dfrac{1}{9} - 5\dfrac{7}{9} = ?$

4. How many quarts are in 7 gallons?

5. Write the ratio 6:14 another way and then put it in simplest form.

6. 5 tablespoons contains how many teaspoons?

7. In a bag of marbles, 3 are blue, 2 are white, 2 are red and 1 is black. Give the probability of picking a blue one? Black? Green?

8. All four sided shapes are called _____.

9. $34,067 - 21,988 = ?$

10. $0.8 - 0.4673 = ?$

11. Round 34,568,992 to the nearest thousand.

12. Figures with the same size and the same shape are _____.

13. Which digit is in the thousandths place in 35.981?

14. Kerry bought 2 pairs of tennis shoes that cost $42 a pair. The store was having a sale: $25 off the price of a second pair of shoes. How much did Kerry pay for both pairs of shoes?

15. $81,252 \div 6 = ?$

16. Solve for n. $\dfrac{3}{8} = \dfrac{9}{n}$

17. There are 12 girls and 15 boys. What is the boy-girl ratio?

18. During which month did the greatest amount of snow fall?

19. About how many inches of snow fell during the whole five months?

20. In which months did 6 in. of snow fall?

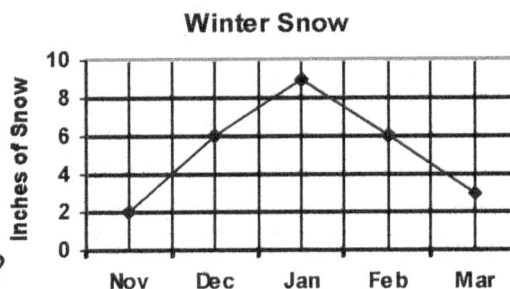

1.

2.

3.

4.

5.

6.

7.

8.

9.

10.

11.

12.

13.

14.

15.

16.

17.

18.

19.

20.

Lesson #115

1. What temperature is shown on the thermometer?

2. If $5x = 30$, what is the value of x?

3. What is the probability of a coin landing heads-up on one toss of the coin?

4. $5.62 + 0.8 + 3.0 = ?$

5. $3,888 \div 36 = ?$

6. $0.007 \times 0.009 = ?$

7. $208.4 \div 0.8 = ?$

8. How many cups are in 6 pints?

9. $1\dfrac{1}{3} + 1\dfrac{1}{6} = ?$

10. $\dfrac{5}{6} \times \dfrac{12}{25} = ?$

11. Find the GCF of 15 and 25.

12. Draw an obtuse angle? Does it measure more or less than 90°?

13. $34,702 \times 4 = ?$

14. Make a factor tree for 20.

15. Find the range and the mode of 18, 25, 15, 29 and 18.

16. Is 53 a prime or a composite number?

17. Draw a rectangle and shade $\dfrac{2}{5}$ of it.

18. Write $\dfrac{65}{7}$ as a mixed number.

19. Put these fractions in order from least to greatest. $\dfrac{2}{3}, \dfrac{1}{6}, \dfrac{2}{9}$.

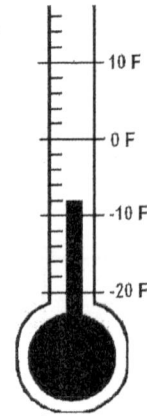

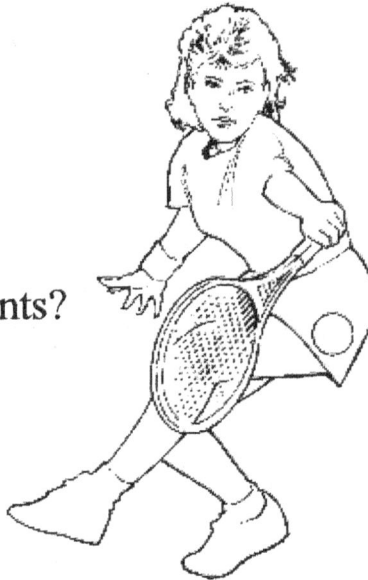

20. $9 - 3\dfrac{3}{5} = ?$

1.

2.

3.

4.

5.

6.

7.

8.

9.

10.

11.

12.

13.

14.

15.

16.

17.

18.

19.

20.

Lesson #116

1. What is the probability of guessing the right answer to a multiple-choice question if the possible answers are a, b, c and d?

2. Find $\dfrac{4}{5}$ of 20.

3. Find 60% of 50.

4. Find the perimeter and the area of this rectangle.

12 in · 6 in

5. What is the name for the number that occurs most often in a list?

6. Write $4\dfrac{5}{6}$ as an improper fraction.

7. $\dfrac{4}{9} \bigcirc \dfrac{7}{10}$

8. Find the LCM of 16 and 20.

9. $\dfrac{5}{8} + \dfrac{3}{8} = ?$

10. $\dfrac{2}{3} \times \dfrac{3}{10} = ?$

11. $\dfrac{48}{8} \div \dfrac{3}{8} = ?$

12. On a Celsius thermometer, water boils at _____.

13. On a Fahrenheit thermometer, water boils at _____.

14. How many centimeters are in 30 meters?

15. Would the more reasonable unit of measure for a bottle of shampoo be milliliters or liters?

16. Shapes made up of line segments are called _____.

17. Write $\dfrac{6}{100}$ as a percent.

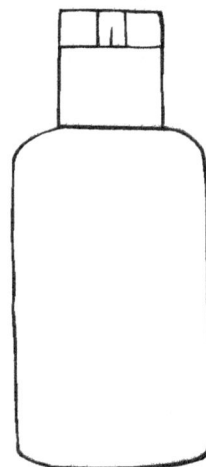

For 18-20, write whether each is a slide, a rotation or a reflection.

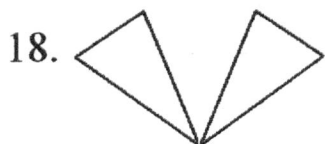

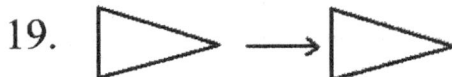

18.   19.   20.

1.

2.

3.

4.

5.

6.

7.

8.

9.

10.

11.

12.

13.

14.

15.

16.

17.

18.

19.

20.

Lesson #117

1.   Identify the name of this shape.

2. $14,580 \div 9 = ?$

3.   Find the average of 52, 34, 62, 23, 71 and 52.

4.   Find the mode of the set of numbers in problem #3.

5.   Write the formula for finding the area of a rectangle.

6. $34.7 + 9.87 + 0.764 = ?$

7.   The area of a square is 36 in^2. What is the length of each side?

8.   Give the estimated difference of 653 and 341.

9.   Find $\dfrac{4}{5}$ of 40.

10.   Solve to find the value of x. $\dfrac{x}{4} = \dfrac{27}{36}$

11.   In a bag of marbles, 4 are red, 6 are white and 10 are green. What is the red-white ratio? the white-green ratio? the red-green ratio?

12.   Kendra went to the store and bought apples for $1.30, bread for $0.99 and 3 cans of pop for $0.80 each. He was given $5.35 in change. How much money did he give the cashier?

13.   Write $\dfrac{4}{5}$ as a decimal and as a percent.

14.   How many feet are in 7 miles?

15.   0.3 $\bigcirc$ 0.12

16. $0.48 \div 8 = ?$

17.   Give the standard number. $(6 \times 1,000) + (7 \times 100) + (4 \times 10) + (3 \times 1)$

18.   Find the LCM of 6, 8 and 12.

19.   What fraction were absent, if $\dfrac{3}{5}$ of the students were present?

20.   Find the volume of this prism.

20 mm

10 mm

30 mm

1.	2.	3.	4.
5.	6.	7.	8.
9.	10.	11.	12.
13.	14.	15.	16.
17.	18.	19.	20.

Lesson #118

1. How many pounds are in $7\frac{1}{2}$ tons?

2. $\frac{6}{7} \bigcirc \frac{9}{11}$

3. Find $\frac{2}{3}$ of 36.

4. $\frac{4}{5} + \frac{1}{4} = ?$

5. If there were 16 sparrows and 12 bluebirds in the aviary, what was the sparrow-bluebird ratio?

6. Find 40% of 60.

7. Write 0.8 as a fraction and as a percent.

8. Find the difference of $\frac{3}{4}$ and $\frac{2}{5}$.

9. How many nickels are in $3?

10. Find the perimeter of an equilateral triangle if a side is 25 mm.

11. $2 \div 3\frac{1}{2} = ?$

12. If $6x = 24$, what is the value of x?

13. Solve for a. $\frac{12}{15} = \frac{a}{20}$

14. $34.56 + 2.789 + 23.9 = ?$

15. Sue made 4 dozen cookies and ate $\frac{1}{6}$ of them. How many are left?

16. How many millimeters are 4 meters?

17. If it is 4:45 now, what time will it be in 6 hours and 10 minutes?

18. Don is 6 feet 3 inches tall. What is Don's height in inches?

19. Is 41 a prime or a composite number?

20. $0.14 \times 0.16 = ?$

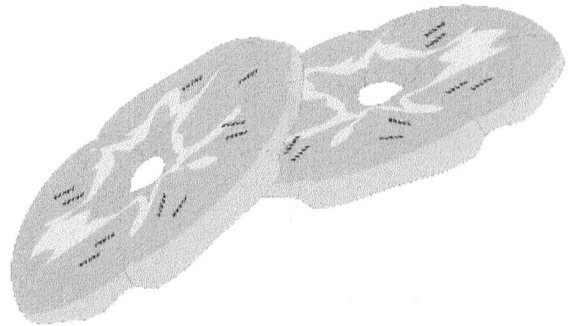

1.

2.

3.

4.

5.

6.

7.

8.

9.

10.

11.

12.

13.

14.

15.

16.

17.

18.

19.

20.

Lesson #119

1. Which factors of 14 are also factors of 21?

2. Numbers that have only two factors are _____ numbers.

3. $(44 + 45) - (20 \times 3) = ?$

4. $4\dfrac{1}{6} - 1\dfrac{5}{6} = ?$

5. Write the number 34,897 in expanded notation.

6. $\dfrac{5}{6} \times \dfrac{2}{3} = ?$

7. Round 35.763 to the nearest tenth.

8. Find the average of 2.4, 5.7 and 6.3.

9. Write 9.3121 in words.

10. If you sleep 8 hours a day, what fraction of the day do you sleep?

11. Find the area of a square if a side measures 13 inches.

12. Find $\dfrac{5}{6}$ of 24.

13. What is the sum of the first five even numbers?

14. $456 - ? = 279$

15. Find the LCM of 16 and 18.

16. Write the reciprocal of $\dfrac{3}{4}$.

17. Which digit is in the thousandths place in 3.790?

18. Arrange these decimals in order from greatest to least.
    3.9   3.009   3.87   3.08

19. Make a factor tree for 64.

20. What is the probability of rolling a seven on one throw of a die?

1.

2.

3.

4.

5.

6.

7.

8.

9.

10.

11.

12.

13.

14.

15.

16.

17.

18.

19.

20.

Lesson #120

1. How many minutes are in 7 hours?

2. Write $\dfrac{3}{10}$ as a decimal and a percent.

3. A triangle with no sides congruent is labeled _____.

4. $0.54 \div 0.06 = ?$

5. $3.45 \times 0.7 = ?$

6. $\dfrac{9}{10} - \dfrac{1}{10} = ?$

7. Find the GCF of 16 and 30.

8. Write $\dfrac{36}{7}$ as a mixed number.

9. How many years are in 5 decades?

10. What is 70% of 30?

11. Find the average of 16, 18, 20 and 22.

12. Write the number 45,679 in words.

13. $244 \div 6 = ?$

14. What is the probability of an event that is certain to happen?

15. A triangle with two sides congruent is called _____.

16. Find the volume of a rectangular prism whose length is 5 feet, whose width is 3 feet, and whose height is 3 feet.

17. Draw a hexagon. Show a line of symmetry.

18. How much money do most students receive?

19. About how many students earn $6 per week?

20. How many students earn less than $5 each week?

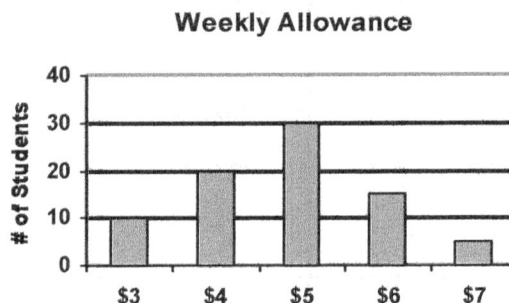

Weekly Allowance

1.

2.

3.

4.

5.

6.

7.

8.

9.

10.

11.

12.

13.

14.

15.

16.

17.

18.

19.

20.

Lesson #121

1. How many centimeters are in 10 meters?

2. Find the median and the mode of 63, 47, 19, 86 and 19.

3. Closed figures made up of line segments are _____.

4. If the radius of a circle is 12 cm, what is the diameter?

5. In Spanish club, the boy-girl ratio was 12 to 15. If 30 girls were members, how many boys were there?

6. Find the area of a square if one side measures 14 inches.

7. Draw a ray.

8. Write 0.6 as a reduced fraction and as a percent.

9. $0.072 \times 1.6 = ?$

10. $\dfrac{5}{10} + \dfrac{2}{5} = ?$

11. Write the ratio 'five to nine' in two other ways.

12. $8,642 + 36,493 = ?$

13. A number with only two factors is a _____ number.

14. Find $\dfrac{3}{5}$ of 15.

15. What is 60% of 80.

16. $7.2 - 3.967 = ?$

17. Write 5.4273 using words.

18. What percent of 50 is 15?

19. Round 46,388,910 to the nearest thousand.

20. $800 - 656 = ?$

1.	2.	3.	4.
5.	6.	7.	8.
9.	10.	11.	12.
13.	14.	15.	16.
17.	18.	19.	20.

Lesson #122

1. Find the LCM of 12 and 18.

2. How many ounces are in 5 pounds?

3. A triangle with all sides congruent is called _____.

4. $3\dfrac{5}{6} + 2\dfrac{2}{3} = ?$

5. How many sides does a pentagon have?

6. Which digit is in the thousandths place in 7.2654?

7. $\dfrac{9}{10} \div \dfrac{3}{10} = ?$

8. Would milliliters or liters be the more reasonable unit for measuring water in a swimming pool?

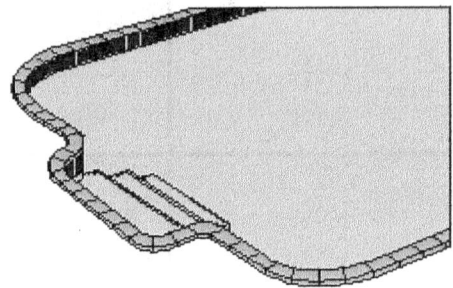

9. The answer in a subtraction problem is called the _____.

10. $97.65 + 34.9 = ?$

11. Estimate the product of 86 and 73.

12. How many nickels are in $3?

13. $\dfrac{6}{10} \times \dfrac{5}{9} = ?$

14. Find the volume of this rectangular prism.

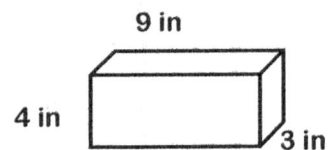

    9 in / 4 in / 3 in

15. Figures with the same size and shape are _____?

16. How many inches are in 4 feet?

17. Find the GCF of 12 and 20.

18. Make a factor tree for 36.

19. Find the area of a square if one side measures 9 feet.

20. How long is this segment?

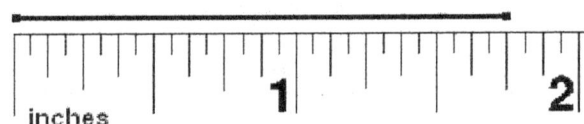

    inches   1   2

1.

2.

3.

4.

5.

6.

7.

8.

9.

10.

11.

12.

13.

14.

15.

16.

17.

18.

19.

20.

Lesson #123

1. The plans for the shed were drawn so that 1 inch = 3 feet. On the plans, the shed is 5 inches tall, how tall will the real shed be?

2. What is the area of a room that is 12 feet long by 10 feet wide?

3. What is 70% of 50?

4. $\dfrac{5}{8} \bigcirc \dfrac{9}{10}$

5. Write $\dfrac{2}{5}$ as a decimal and as a percent.

6. Solve the proportion for x. $\dfrac{6}{10} = \dfrac{9}{x}$

7. Find 15% of 20.

8. How many quarts are in 8 gallons?

9. $1\dfrac{2}{5} + 4\dfrac{2}{3} = ?$

10. What kind of angle measures less than 90°?

11. Round 6.742 to the nearest tenth.

12. How many tons are 14,000 pounds?

13. List the factors of 20.

14. Put $\dfrac{15}{25}$ in simplest form.

15. Draw intersecting lines.

16. $\dfrac{5}{8} \times \dfrac{4}{5} = ?$

17. Is the number 23 prime or composite?

18. Jack is 5 feet 8 inches tall. How many inches tall is Jack?

19. Order these decimals from least to greatest. 6.9, 6.09, 6.19 and 6.7

20. Bill plans to buy a movie ticket for himself and three of his friends. The cost of a ticket is $5.75. How much will Bill spend on tickets?

1.

2.

3.

4.

5.

6.

7.

8.

9.

10.

11.

12.

13.

14.

15.

16.

17.

18.

19.

20.

Lesson #124

1. $0.4 - 0.276 = ?$

2. $0.525 \div 0.05 = ?$

3. $2 - 1\dfrac{1}{5} = ?$

4. Find the GCF of 12 and 18.

5. What is the probability of rolling a six on one throw of a die?

6. What is 20% of 50?

7. How many minutes are in 5 hours?

8. A hot-air balloon flies at a height of 2,561 feet. An airplane is flying 26,784 feet higher than the balloon. How high is the airplane flying?

9. Write 50% as a decimal and as a reduced fraction.

10. Find $\dfrac{1}{6}$ of 24.

11. Are these figures similar or congruent?

12. The answer to a division problem is the _____.

13. Round 23,907,224 to the nearest hundred.

14. What percent of 60 is 18?

15. $45.8 + 9.367 = ?$

16. Put $\dfrac{8}{10}$ in simplest form.

17. Convert 320 ounces into pounds.

18. How many yards are in a mile?

19. Draw perpendicular lines.

20. In a class of 30 students, there are 14 boys. What is the boy-girl ratio in the class?

1.

2.

3.

4.

5.

6.

7.

8.

9.

10.

11.

12.

13.

14.

15.

16.

17.

18.

19.

20.

Lesson #125

1. How many centimeters are in 4 meters?

2. $\dfrac{5}{8} \bigcirc \dfrac{7}{11}$

3. Find $\dfrac{4}{5}$ of 40.

4. $27 \times 34 = ?$

5. A triangle with two congruent sides is a(n) _____.

6. Write $\dfrac{34}{6}$ as a mixed number.

7. $0.5 \div 2.5 = ?$

8. $8\dfrac{1}{4} - 5\dfrac{3}{4} = ?$

9. Round 3.982 to the nearest hundredth.

10. Make a factor tree for 24.

11. $\dfrac{7}{10} - \dfrac{1}{2} = ?$

12. $\dfrac{8}{10} \div \dfrac{4}{10} = ?$

13. Write 45% as a decimal and a reduced fraction.

14. 70% of what number is 35?

15. Which factors of 12 are also factors of 24?

16. Find the perimeter of a hexagon if each side measures 12 inches.

17. Give the probability of rolling a 1, 2 or 3 on one roll of a die?

18. $20.25 \div 0.5 = ?$

19. If the quotient is 9 and the dividend is 72, what is the divisor?

20. State whether the figure was moved by a rotation, a slide or a reflection.

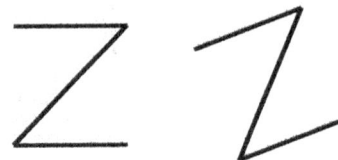

1.	2.	3.	4.
5.	6.	7.	8.
9.	10.	11.	12.
13.	14.	15.	16.
17.	18.	19.	20.

Lesson #126

1.　Draw a cube. How many faces does it have?

2.　If it is 5:20 now, what time was it 6 hours and 10 minutes ago?

3.　$\dfrac{5}{6} \times \dfrac{3}{5} = ?$

4.　$3 - 1\dfrac{1}{8} = ?$

5.　If $7x = 42$, what is the value of x?

6.　$0.5 - 0.3682 = ?$

7.　How many centuries are 600 years?

8.　Write $2\dfrac{4}{5}$ as an improper fraction.

9.　Find the average of 2.4, 6.3 and 5.7.

10.　Write 568,932 in expanded notation.

11.　Find the LCM of 10 and 15.

12.　$0.009 \times 0.05 = ?$

13.　Find the area of this rectangle.

10 cm

13 cm

14.　$4{,}283 \div 9 = ?$

15.　Solve the proportion for x.　$\dfrac{8}{10} = \dfrac{12}{x}$

16.　What is the name of this shape?

17.　Find 40% of 70.

18.　What percent of 80 is 24?

19.　Find the value of c.　$\dfrac{4}{6} = \dfrac{12}{c}$

20.　$\dfrac{9}{11} - \dfrac{3}{11} = ?$

1.

2.

3.

4.

5.

6.

7.

8.

9.

10.

11.

12.

13.

14.

15.

16.

17.

18.

19.

20.

Lesson #127

1. What is the value of x? $\dfrac{3}{8} = \dfrac{9}{x}$

2. $\dfrac{5}{8} + \dfrac{3}{8} = ?$

3. How many millimeters are 7 meters?

4. Give the probability of rolling an even number on one roll of a die.

5. Write 12% as a decimal and a reduced fraction.

6. Write the ratio $\dfrac{7}{9}$ in two other ways.

7. Find the GCF of 14 and 21.

8. $7.5 \div 0.5 = ?$

9. $4 - 2\dfrac{5}{7} = ?$

10. Find the volume of a rectangular prism if its length is 8 meters, its width is 5 meters and its height is 3 meters.

11. $0.9 - 0.8643 = ?$

12. 40% of what number is 28?

13. Draw a ray.

14. The radius of a circle is 17 centimeters. What is the diameter?

15. Find the median and the mode of 56, 77, 89, 32 and 77.

16. Find $\dfrac{3}{5}$ of 60.

17. The area of a square is 49 ft^2. What is the length of each side?

18. What is 15% of 60.

19. Draw two similar pentagons.

20. What time will it be in 9 hours and 25 minutes, if it is 7:10 now?

1.

2.

3.

4.

5.

6.

7.

8.

9.

10.

11.

12.

13.

14.

15.

16.

17.

18.

19.

20.

Lesson #128

1. $\dfrac{5}{12} \bigcirc \dfrac{7}{11}$

2. Find the estimated sum of 6,788 and 4,321.

3. Make a factor tree for 30.

4. $45,677 + 98,249 = ?$

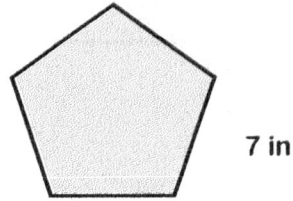

5. Find the perimeter of this pentagon.   7 in

6. $90,000 - 34,761 = ?$

7. What number is next in this sequence? 45, 54, 63, ...

8. $0.089 \times 0.04 = ?$

9. Write 0.12 as a reduced fraction.

10. $0.3 \bigcirc 0.24$.

11. How many cups are in 10 pints?

12. $\dfrac{9}{4} \div 1\dfrac{1}{2} = ?$

13. Draw a right angle. How many degrees are in a right angle?

14. Marcus sleeps 8 hours each night. What fraction of the day does Marcus sleep?

15. List the factors of 24.

16. Round 56.752 to the nearest tenth.

17. Write 9.679 in words.

18. Carl bought 10 bottles of correction fluid at a price of $0.35 each. How much was his bill?

19. Write $\dfrac{67}{8}$ as a mixed number.

20. $29 \times 35 = ?$

1.

2.

3.

4.

5.

6.

7.

8.

9.

10.

11.

12.

13.

14.

15.

16.

17.

18.

19.

20.

Lesson #129

1. What is 70% of 30?

2. Find the perimeter of the octagon.

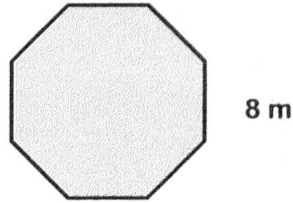

8 m

3. $6 - 3\frac{3}{7} = ?$

4. $0.12 \times 0.05 = ?$

5. $82.40 \div 0.04 = ?$

6. If $5x = 35$, what is the value of x?

7. $\frac{9}{12}$ ◯ $\frac{8}{11}$

8. Find $\frac{3}{5}$ of 20.

9. $\frac{5}{8} \times \frac{12}{15} = ?$

10. Find the LCM of 12 and 20.

11. How many inches are in 5 yards?

12. Find the median of 36, 17, 29, 73 and 54.

13. Round 34.67 to the nearest tenth.

14. $36 \times 58 = ?$

15. Solve for the value of x. $\frac{9}{12} = \frac{x}{60}$

16. Write 3.736 in words.

17. It is 5:25. What time was it 6 hours and 10 minutes ago?

18. Write 0.55 as a percent and as a reduced fraction.

19. Sue is 5 feet 8 inches tall. How many inches tall is Sue?

20. Make a factor tree for 18.

1.

2.

3.

4.

5.

6.

7.

8.

9.

10.

11.

12.

13.

14.

15.

16.

17.

18.

19.

20.

Lesson #130

1. $0.06 \bigcirc 0.052$.

2. $863,422 + 36,849 = ?$

3. Find the probability of rolling an odd number on one roll of a die.

4. $0.6 - 0.4275 = ?$

5. Find the area of a square whose side measures 12 inches.

6. Write 14% as a decimal and as a reduced fraction.

7. Write $\dfrac{52}{8}$ as a mixed number.

8. Draw perpendicular lines.

9. Round 42,465,232 to the nearest thousand.

10. What is the name of this shape?

11. Find the value of x. $\dfrac{12}{15} = \dfrac{x}{20}$

12. How many years are 12 decades?

13. $6\dfrac{2}{5} + 3\dfrac{1}{4} = ?$

14. Write $3\dfrac{3}{5}$ as an improper fraction.

15. 70% of what number is 28?

16. Find the mode and the range of 32, 57, 98, 46 and 57.

17. How many centuries are 500 years?

18. $3.6 \times 0.04 = ?$

19. Find the average of 63, 47 and 70.

20. Sharon had 60 pieces of candy. She gave $\dfrac{1}{5}$ to her brother and $\dfrac{3}{5}$ of the candy to her best friend. How many pieces of candy did Sharon have left?

1.

2.

3.

4.

5.

6.

7.

8.

9.

10.

11.

12.

13.

14.

15.

16.

17.

18.

19.

20.

Lesson #131

1.   Find the GCF and LCM of 8 and 12.

2.   What is the value of x? $\dfrac{5}{6} = \dfrac{40}{x}$

3.   Write $\dfrac{7}{8}$ as a decimal and as a percent.

4. $36,724 \div 4 = ?$

5.   How many hours are 2,400 minutes?

6.   Write 6,379,486 in expanded form.

7.   Find $\dfrac{2}{3}$ of 90.

8.   What is 20% of 50?

9.   Figures with the same shape but different sizes are _____?

10. $\dfrac{6}{10} \times \dfrac{8}{12} = ?$

11.   Draw an acute angle.

12.   Find the volume of this rectangular prism.

4 m
8 m
3 m

13.   In a bag of marbles, there are 3 white, 2 blue, 2 green and 1 black. Give the probability of picking a white marble? Black? Blue?

14.   How many pounds are $9\dfrac{1}{2}$ tons?

15.   Put these decimals in order from greatest to least.
      3.072   3.7   3.027   3.02.

16.   Write the time 8 minutes before noon.

17.   List the factors of 16.

18. $0.006 \times 0.004 = ?$

19.   If the diameter of a circle is 22 inches, what is the radius?

20.   The ratio of boys to girls on the bus is 4 to 3. If there were 16 boys, how many girls are on the bus?

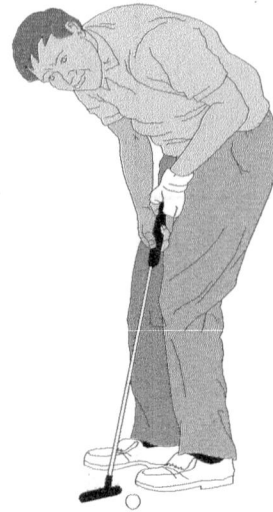

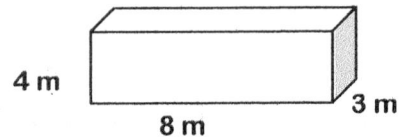

1.	2.	3.	4.
5.	6.	7.	8.
9.	10.	11.	12.
13.	14.	15.	16.
17.	18.	19.	20.

Lesson #132

1. Draw a straight angle. How many degrees are in a straight angle?

2. $4\frac{1}{2} \times 2\frac{1}{3} = ?$

3. Round 37.624 to the nearest hundredth.

4. $\frac{4}{7} \times \frac{14}{16} = ?$

5. Write 50% as a decimal and as a reduced fraction.

6. Write 6.3752 in words.

7. What type of shape is shown?

8. Write the ratio 6:11 in two other ways.

9. $\frac{3}{5} \bigcirc \frac{4}{9}$

10. This week, Marquis drove 13 miles on Monday, 17 miles on Tuesday, 21 miles on Wednesday and 25 miles on Thursday. If this pattern continues, how far will he drive next Wednesday?

11. $\frac{8}{10} \div \frac{4}{10} = ?$

12. $24.86 \div 0.02 = ?$

13. What percent of 80 is 24?

14. Draw parallel lines.

15. A class of 60 students ate 15 pizzas. How many pizzas would be needed for 120 students?

16. $86.2 + 37.563 = ?$

17. Find the LCM of 6 and 15.

18. How many quarts are in 8 gallons?

19. Closed figures made up of line segments are _____.

20. On a Celsius thermometer, water boils at _____.

1.

2.

3.

4.

5.

6.

7.

8.

9.

10.

11.

12.

13.

14.

15.

16.

17.

18.

19.

20.

Lesson #133

1. $9\dfrac{3}{7} - 6\dfrac{6}{7} = ?$

2. On the Fahrenheit scale, water freezes at _____.

3. Write 42,654 in expanded form.

4. Solve the proportion for x. $\dfrac{8}{12} = \dfrac{6}{x}$

5. Write 0.16 as a fraction and as a percent.

6. Find the average of 65, 30 and 25.

7. $60,000 - 27,988 = ?$

8. An eight-sided shape is a(n) _____.

9. Draw a right angle. How many degrees are in a right angle?

10. $4,862 \times 5 = ?$

11. $3.06 \bigcirc 3.006$

12. Numbers that have only 2 factors are _____ numbers.

13. Find the GCF of 15 and 25.

14. $0.05 \times 0.04 = ?$

15. What is the probability of rolling a 2 on one roll of a die?

16. Find the area of a rectangle if the length is 15 millimeters and the width is 7 millimeters.

17. What will be the time 90 minutes after noon?

18. $8\dfrac{1}{5} + 4\dfrac{1}{2} = ?$

19. Find $\dfrac{2}{5}$ of 40.

20. Write $3\dfrac{2}{3}$ as an improper fraction.

1.

2.

3.

4.

5.

6.

7.

8.

9.

10.

11.

12.

13.

14.

15.

16.

17.

18.

19.

20.

Lesson #134

1. On the Celsius scale, at what temperature does water freeze?

2. List the first 5 prime numbers.

3. $\dfrac{8}{10} \times \dfrac{12}{16} = ?$

4. Draw intersecting lines.

5. Write $\dfrac{34}{6}$ as a mixed number.

6. Find the volume of this rectangular prism.

10 m

2 m

5 m

7. Make a factor tree for 50.

8. $0.4 - 0.163 = ?$

9. $12 - 8\dfrac{4}{5} = ?$

10. List the factors of 24.

11. Find the area of a square if a side measures 8 yards.

12. Write the reciprocal of $\dfrac{5}{8}$.

13. Round 3.786 to the nearest tenth.

14. Write $\dfrac{7}{10}$ as a decimal and as a percent.

15. $86 + 25 + 47 = ?$

16. How many feet are in 4 miles?

17. Write the next two numbers in the sequence. 25, 31, 37, …

18. Put $\dfrac{12}{15}$ in simplest form.

19. Write $\dfrac{2}{5}$ as a decimal.

20. A triangle with all congruent sides is a(n) _____ triangle.

1.

2.

3.

4.

5.

6.

7.

8.

9.

10.

11.

12.

13.

14.

15.

16.

17.

18.

19.

20.

Lesson #135

1. $\dfrac{9}{10} - \dfrac{2}{3} = ?$

2. It is 6:30. What time will it be in 80 minutes?

3. Round 36,475,039 to the nearest million.

4. How many decades are in 50 years?

5. Jerry is 6 feet 2 inches tall. What is Jerry's height in inches?

6. Write 14.026 in words.

7. Find $\dfrac{3}{5}$ of 20.

8. $36.7 + 94.82 = ?$

9. 600 centimeters are how many meters?

10. Find 80% of 30.

11. Find the value of x. $\dfrac{5}{8} = \dfrac{30}{x}$

12. Write 65% as a reduced fraction.

13. If $9x = 27$, what is the value of x?

14. $3.4 \times 2.6 = ?$

15. Which digit is in the ten thousands place in 6,473,295?

16. Is 46 a prime or a composite number?

17. Draw an obtuse angle.

18. Make a factor tree for 28.

19. If the radius of a circle is 15 inches, what is the diameter?

20. Put $\dfrac{20}{25}$ in simplest form.

1.

2.

3.

4.

5.

6.

7.

8.

9.

10.

11.

12.

13.

14.

15.

16.

17.

18.

19.

20.

Lesson #136

1. $45.05 \div 0.05 = ?$

2. $700 - 463 = ?$

3.   Solve for x. $\dfrac{4}{5} = \dfrac{x}{60}$

4.   On the Fahrenheit scale, water boils at _____.

5. $1\dfrac{3}{5} + 4\dfrac{3}{4} = ?$

6.   What is 90% of 40?

7. $7.3 - 5.836 = ?$

8.   Which digit is in the thousandths place in 17.375?

9.   Write 60% as a decimal and as a reduced fraction.

10. Put 1.6, 1.062 and 1.006, in order from least to greatest.

11. $14\dfrac{1}{8} - 10\dfrac{5}{8} = ?$

13 cm

12. $0.012 \times 0.07 = ?$

5 cm

13. Find the perimeter.

14. Figures with the same size and shape are _____.

15. $\dfrac{8}{9} \times \dfrac{3}{16} = ?$

16. $93{,}475 + 46{,}288 = ?$

17. Find the GCF and the LCM of 12 and 18.

18. Write 7.62 in words.

19. Write the reciprocal of $\dfrac{12}{15}$.

20. How many cups are in 7 pints?

1.

2.

3.

4.

5.

6.

7.

8.

9.

10.

11.

12.

13.

14.

15.

16.

17.

18.

19.

20.

Lesson #137

1. A triangle with no congruent sides is a(n) _____triangle.

2. $3\frac{1}{5} + 4\frac{3}{10} = ?$

3. How many centimeters are in 15 meters?

4. If $8x = 72$, what is the value of x?

5. The area of a square is 64 square feet. How long is each side?

6. $2.8 - 0.9742 = ?$

7. Find $\frac{4}{5}$ of 25.

8. The boy-girl ratio at the park was 9 to 7. If there were 54 boys, how many girls were at the park?

9. $7 - 2\frac{3}{5} = ?$

10. How many centuries are between 1570 and 1970?

11. Sam and his sister are putting their money together to buy a cell phone that costs $99.89. Sam has $36.55 and his sister has $32.49. How much more money do they need in order to buy the phone?

12. Give the name of this polygon.

13. Write $\frac{3}{10}$ as a decimal and as a percent.

14. $\frac{6}{7} \bigcirc \frac{5}{8}$

15. How many millimeters are 4 meters?

16. $3 \div 7\frac{1}{2} = ?$

17. Draw parallel lines.

18. Which factors of 12 are also factors of 24?

19. In Fahrenheit, at what temperature does water boil?

20. Make a factor tree for 18.

1.

2.

3.

4.

5.

6.

7.

8.

9.

10.

11.

12.

13.

14.

15.

16.

17.

18.

19.

20.

Lesson #138

1. Write $3\frac{4}{7}$ as an improper fraction.

2. Closed figures made up of line segments are _____.

3. Write $\frac{1}{3}$ as a decimal.

4. What is the 5th prime number?

5. Identify the name of this shape.

6. A regular octagon has a perimeter of 56 in. How long is each side?

7. Which is the more reasonable measurement for the height of a ceiling, 8 feet or 8 yards?

8. $8\frac{3}{5} - 4\frac{4}{5} = ?$

9. What percent of 60 is 42?

10. Find the average of 1.3, 2.0 and 0.81.

11. $24 \div 0.08 = ?$

12. Find the median of the numbers 67, 89, 20, 44 and 16.

13. What is the range of the set of numbers in problem #12?

14. Six of 30 students earned a B on the math test. What fraction of the students got a B on the test? What percent of students got a B?

15. Clay had 75 crayons. He gave $\frac{2}{5}$ of them to his sister and $\frac{1}{5}$ of them to his little brother. How many crayons did Clay have left?

16. Draw a ray.

17. $50,000 - 27,886 = ?$

18. It is 9:15. What time was it 7 hours and 5 minutes ago?

19. Find the LCM of 14 and 16.

20. Find the volume of this figure in cm^3.

1.

2.

3.

4.

5.

6.

7.

8.

9.

10.

11.

12.

13.

14.

15.

16.

17.

18.

19.

20.

Lesson #139

1. $345,667 + 29,726 = ?$

2. Find the GCF of 14 and 21.

3. How many inches are in 6 feet?

4. $0.8 - 0.6773 = ?$

5. $\dfrac{5}{8} \times \dfrac{2}{3} = ?$

6. List the factors of 20.

7. $2,025 \div 25 = ?$

8. Which digit is in the hundredths place in 5.602?

9. Round 35,690,552 to the nearest thousand.

10. What is the answer to a subtraction problem called?

11. Find the perimeter of a rectangle whose length is 12 meters and whose width is 5 meters.

12. Find $\dfrac{5}{6}$ of 30.

13. 70% of what number is 35?

14. Write 0.15 as a percent and as a reduced fraction.

15. A triangle with 2 sides congruent is a(n) _____ triangle.

16. If $5n = 45$, what is the value of n?

17. Round 34.744 to the nearest tenth.

18. $0.009 \times 0.06 = ?$

19. Write the ratio 12:19 in two other ways.

20. Name this shape.

1.

2.

3.

4.

5.

6.

7.

8.

9.

10.

11.

12.

13.

14.

15.

16.

17.

18.

19.

20.

Lesson #140

1. How many gallons are 28 quarts?

2. $0.7 - 0.3326 = ?$

3. $\dfrac{4}{7} \bigcirc \dfrac{10}{11}$

4. $\dfrac{6}{10} \div \dfrac{2}{10} = ?$

5. Find the perimeter of a square if one side measures 13 meters.

6. The radius of a circle is 14 mm. What is the diameter?

7. The temperature was 12° at noon. By 9:00 p.m., it dropped by 15°. What was the temperature at 9:00 p.m.?

8. How many degrees are in a right angle?

9. Write $\dfrac{15}{2}$ as a mixed number.

10. Write $\dfrac{3}{20}$ as a decimal and as a percent.

11. 90% of what number is 63?

12. Round 90,867,552 to the nearest hundred thousand.

13. Draw a ray.

14. On the Fahrenheit temperature scale, water boils at _____.

15. If $12x = 36$, what is the value of x?

16. Make a factor tree for 45.

17. How many inches are in 2 yards?

18. $7,890,654 + 3,442,897 = ?$

19. What is the probability of drawing a jack out of a deck of 52 cards?

20. Marilyn is 5 feet 7 inches tall. How many inches tall is Marilyn?

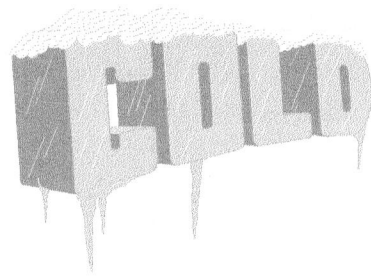

1.

2.

3.

4.

5.

6.

7.

8.

9.

10.

11.

12.

13.

14.

15.

16.

17.

18.

19.

20.